ON SOCIAL JUSTICE

St Basil the Great

ST VLADIMIR'S SEMINARY PRESS
Popular Patristics Series
Number 38

The Popular Patristics Series published by St Vladimir's Seminary Press provides readable and accurate translations of a wide range of early Christian literature to a wide audience—students of Christian history to lay Christians reading for spiritual benefit. Recognized scholars in their fields provide short but comprehensive and clear introductions to the material. The texts include classics of Christian literature, thematic volumes, collections of homilies, letters on spiritual counsel, and poetical works from a variety of geographical contexts and historical backgrounds. The mission of the series is to mine the riches of the early Church and to make these treasures available to all.

Series Editor
JOHN BEHR

Associate Editor
NONNA VERNA HARRISON

On Social Justice

ST BASIL THE GREAT

Translation with Introduction
and Commentary by

C. PAUL SCHROEDER

Foreword by Gregory P. Yova

ST VLADIMIR'S SEMINARY PRESS
CRESTWOOD, NEW YORK
2009

Library of Congress Cataloging-in-Publication Data

Basil, Saint, Bishop of Caesarea, ca. 329–379.
    [Selections. English, 2009]
    On social justice / St. Basil the Great ; translation with introduction and
commentary by C. Paul Schroeder ; foreword by Gregory P. Yova.
        p. cm. — (Popular patristics series, 1555–5755 ; no. 38)
        Includes bibliographical references.
        ISBN 978-0-88141-053-2
        1. Social justice—Religious aspects—Christianity. 2. Christianity and justice.
    3. Theology—History—Early church, ca. 30–600. I. Schroeder, C. Paul. II. Title.

    BR65.B33E6 2009
    201'.7—dc22

                                                            2009031773

COPYRIGHT © 2009 BY

ST VLADIMIR'S SEMINARY PRESS
575 Scarsdale Road, Crestwood, NY 10707
1-800-204-2665
www.svspress.com

ISBN 978-088141-053-2
ISSN 1555-5755

PRINTED IN THE UNITED STATES OF AMERICA

Para mis hermanos y hermanas
Los trabajadores de Proyecto México y Casa Hogar San Inocencio
Los constructores de la Nueva Ciudad
En el Nuevo Mundo

For my brothers and sisters
The workers of Project Mexico and St Innocent Orphanage
Builders of the New City
In the New World

Contents

Foreword

Have you ever had an overwhelming encounter with a beautiful aspect of God's creation, and then struggled to describe it to others? Have you ever read something so powerful that it forever changed the way you live your life? Have you ever had a truly life-changing experience? Certain events are impossible to explain in mere words. For me, reading the writings of St Basil the Great in the following chapters was one of those experiences: life-changing and indescribable.

After my first visit to Alaska, I was so moved to the core of my being that I wanted to share it with everyone ... but the incredible splendor and vast expanses of untainted beauty were powerful beyond words. The eerie quiet. The "white thunder" of creaking glaciers. The purity of nature with its amazing array of creatures great and small. The glorious breach and crash of a humpback whale. The monstrous power of a calving glacier. The virtual carpet of salmon fighting their way upstream to fulfill their mission. The sunset at midnight. A solitary, soaring bald eagle. My paltry words couldn't begin to convey the reality.

Perhaps you've had a similar experience with an inspiring book, a special meal, or a gorgeous locale. With great confidence, you tell friends that it would be worth the effort to experience it for themselves—but your description falls short. That's how I feel about these writings of Basil. There is no way to describe the power, simplicity, wisdom, and freedom of his words; but just as I would confidently urge my friends to visit Alaska and assure them without a doubt that it would be a blessing to them, so I wholeheartedly recommend this book to you.

When you read Basil's words, you will think they were written yesterday—not 1,600 years ago! It's unbelievable how precisely he describes our modern struggle with material wealth, our responsibility to our fellow man, and how to live a life in balance. The struggle he describes is the exact struggle facing any person with a conscience. How much is enough? How far should I go to provide for my family and myself? What is my responsibility to others? Do I have to "sell everything and give it all to the poor" to make God happy? Basil's guidance in these difficult areas will not only surprise you, it will also feel like a cup of cool water to your soul. When we see suffering and are pained by it, it is the image of God within us yearning to do what we were created to do—to be a child of God and help alleviate that suffering. But we hesitate, and at that moment our own soul suffers, because in order to grow, the soul needs to connect with and give to another. When we don't respond, we not only rob the person in need; we rob ourselves. Basil's words sear the mind and heart, but in the end, they actually make it easier for us to serve others. For if we heed them, we will serve not out of guilt, but out of inspiration from the kind but firm guidance of a wise and loving master which awakens us to a better way. Then we will lead a life that not only enriches others, but also brings sunshine and nourishment to our own hungry souls. We can live truly blessed lives!

Despite the fact that Basil's words feel right to us, my interactions with thousands of people have shown me that even those who are trying to live a life committed to Christ and his teachings are uncertain how to apply these principles in their daily lives. They're aware of the inequities in the world and occasionally feel the emptiness of consumerism or a self-centered existence, but most honestly don't know what to do about it. "Sell all and follow me" comes to mind once in a while and is quickly dismissed. However, as with almost all significant changes, this is a process. No one can do it all at once. We must start the journey by taking *small* steps on a *daily* basis. Basil's words offer the wisdom to help us move forward in a deliberate and meaningful way. He assists us by talking through the litany of obstacles we throw in the path of this blessed life. Unexpectedly, it's very liberating to read his description of the many ways we convince ourselves that we have certain financial "needs." He so eloquently describes the pitfalls and enslavement of living on credit that you'll think he was speaking today.

An unexpected result of this life committed to helping others is that the giver ends up feeling that he or she received more than was given. The common response from thousands of volunteers we've hosted at Project Mexico and St Innocent Orphanage, who have built homes for the poor or assisted at the orphanage, is that they feel they received more than they gave. Our goal has been to give them a taste of serving those in need and then send them home, hopefully to continue reaching out to others in whatever way God leads.

Be forewarned that Basil pulls no punches. He is clear that many of us are actually robbing the poor by our lifestyles. It is at times strong medicine, but there is no angst or bitterness behind it. It stings, but only because it is true and correct, not because he is harsh. Though I have spent the last twenty years dedicated to serving the poor and orphans and teaching others how to do works of mercy, the words of St Basil pierced my heart and revealed how much is yet to be done in my own soul. I thank God for Fr Paul Schroeder's excellent and much-needed translation. In my opinion this is the best work I have ever read about charity, works of mercy, and how to live our lives in balance.

In my lifetime, I've met only a handful of people who are not encumbered by material concerns. They are the ones who simply give whatever is needed and whatever they have with a smile on their faces. Somehow, they seem always to have something to give; their well is constantly refilled. I suspect the rest of us are missing out on the joy and blessings this small group of people enjoys. So the answer for us is to take small steps every day, knowing that as we do so, we become more of what God intended us to be, and thus more peaceful, more joyful, and more of a blessing to those around us.

Gregory P. Yova
Founder, Project Mexico and St Innocent Orthodox Orphanage
June 9, 2007

Preface

One day, as I was in the final stages of completing this book, the timeliness of the project was brought home to me while I was sitting in a salon getting my hair cut. In the next chair over, a woman was having an animated discussion with her stylist. The topic of their conversation was this: In an era of corporate moguls and billionaire CEOs, of superstar athletes and entertainment celebrities, how much of the world's wealth and resources can one person rightfully claim? At the height of the Arian controversy, St Gregory of Nyssa once wryly remarked that the topic of discussion in the shops, the marketplaces, and on every street corner was the question, "Was there a time when the Son was not?"[1] But in our day, the question one is perhaps more likely to hear being debated in hair salons, offices, and grocery store checkout aisles is this: "How much is enough, and how much is too much?"

Perhaps this is why St Basil's homilies on the subject of wealth and poverty seem so utterly fresh and contemporary today. The heart of Basil's message is this: *Simplify your life, so you have something to share with others.* And this offers a place to start for everyone, both those who possess great wealth and those of modest means. Even the poor, as Basil points out, can benefit by sharing. While some patristic texts concern obscure and highly philosophical questions of theology, and thus require significant introductory and explanatory material in order to be understood by the modern reader, Basil's teachings on social issues are for the most part as immediately graspable and applicable today as they were in the fourth century. It may

[1]Gregory of Nyssa *On the Deity of the Son and the Holy Spirit*; J. P. Migne et al, ed. *Patrologia Graeca* (Paris: Migne, 1857), 46:557B (henceforth cited as PG).

even be, at a time when vast income disparity, overuse of limited environmental resources, and global climate change are becoming matters of increasing concern, that Basil's message is more relevant now than ever before.

As Greg Yova, founder of Project Mexico and St Innocent Orphanage, notes in his Foreword to the text, no description can ever substitute for the actual experience of reading Basil's words for oneself. For this reason, the reader may wish initially to skip the Introduction and proceed directly to Basil's homilies, in order to experience firsthand his piercing power of observation and profound ability to persuade and motivate. Afterwards, he or she may wish to return to the Introduction, which provides additional biographical information about Basil, an attempt at synthesis of his thought, and a description of the "New City," the community founded by Basil in response to the pressing social concerns of his day. The process of reading and reflecting on these texts over the past several years has proved personally transformative for me; Basil's words have literally changed my life. It is my prayer that they may do the same for you.

I am deeply grateful to Greg and Margaret Yova for their encouragement throughout the process of translating these texts, as well as their inspirational example in seeking daily to live out the truths expounded herein. It is to them, their co-workers at Project Mexico and St Innocent Orphanage, and all the volunteers who travel to Mexico every year to build homes and work at the orphanage that this volume is lovingly dedicated.

C. Paul Schroeder
July 29, 2007

Introduction

The Two Turnings—Basil's Early Life and Education, Monastic Profession, and Return to Caesarea

St Basil the Great was born in Caesarea of Cappadocia around AD 330 to a prominent Christian family of some renown in the region. His family lineage constitutes a veritable "household of saints": his mother, Emmelia, was the orphaned daughter of a martyred Christian nobleman, while his paternal grandmother, Macrina the Elder, had been instructed by disciples of St Gregory the Wonderworker. His grandmother, his father, and his mother all became saints of the Church, as did four of his nine brothers and sisters. His younger brother Peter became bishop of Sebasteia, and his younger brother Gregory became bishop of Nyssa; Gregory was also a prolific writer and theologian. His older sister Macrina was the first member of the family to embrace the ascetic life; she also appears to have been a theologian in her own right, based upon conversations recorded by her brother Gregory. Later in life, Basil credited the influence of his family, and especially that of his mother and grandmother, as crucial to his own spiritual and theological development.[1]

Basil's family was notable not only for its piety, but also for its wealth and social status. His early life unfolds against a backdrop of significant privilege, a fact that becomes important when examining his later life and his attitudes towards wealth and wealthy people. His

---

[1]On Basil's use of his family lineage as a touchstone of orthodoxy, see Philip Rousseau, *Basil of Caesarea* (Berkeley, CA: University of California Press, 1998), 23–24.

father, Basil the Elder, was a renowned lawyer and rhetorician, and a member of the Roman aristocracy;[2] Basil's name, like that of his father before him, means "royal," suggesting noble birth. Although it is uncertain whether anyone in Basil's family belonged to the senatorial rank, they were clearly among the elite minority of the upper class. Within a social context where wealth was measured primarily in terms of landholdings, Basil's family would have been regarded as prosperous indeed. In addition to properties located in Cappadocia and Pontus, they owned a large country estate in Annisa[3] along the banks of the River Iris, where they often retired for hunting and recreation;[4] it was here that Basil spent much of his childhood. Basil's privileged upbringing makes his writings about how the wealthy live particularly interesting. When he describes their houses, their dress, their occupations and their mannerisms, it is likely that he is drawing, at least in part, from his personal experience in such matters. For example, his homily *To the Rich* contains an impressive description of the leisurely pursuits of the landed aristocracy—hunting, horseback riding, baths in the city and countryside—a life of which Basil would have possessed firsthand knowledge from his youth.[5]

In addition to the financial and social benefits stemming from his family's status, another advantage of Basil's noble birth should also be noted: freedom. In a society where a significant proportion of the population, perhaps one-third,[6] was enslaved, Basil lived as a free

[2]Thomas A. Kopecek concludes that Basil's family belonged to the curial class of the aristocracy; see "The Social Class of the Cappadocian Fathers," *Church History* 42 (1973): 461–66.

[3]Rousseau identifies Annisa as the modern Turkish town of Sonusa (also known as Uluköy); *Basil of Caesarea*, 62 n. 7.

[4]Basil's brother Gregory notes that after the death of their father their mother "was paying taxes to three governors, since her property was scattered throughout that number of provinces." Gregory of Nyssa, *The Life of St Macrina*, Kevin Corrigan, trans. (Saskatoon, Saskatchewan: Peregrina Publishing Co., 1987), 6.

[5]*To the Rich* 2. For a description of aristocratic privilege in Basil's time, see Michele Renee Salzman, *The Making of a Christian Aristocracy: Social and Religious Change in the Western Roman Empire* (Cambridge, MA: Harvard University Press, 2002), 24 ff.

[6]While averring that "the evidence does not permit genuine quantification" of the

man, enjoying a range of opportunities completely inaccessible to those enslaved through capture, birth, or sale. Although slaves were not generally counted among the poor in the ancient world, since their owners were responsible for feeding and clothing them,[7] their lives were hard, their punishments were severe, and their life expectancy was short. Free birth was a privilege in an era when personal freedom was by no means guaranteed. Many slaves were foreign captives, but residents of the empire could also lose their freedom in a variety of ways. People were sold into slavery together with their children in order to pay foreclosed debts, as Basil describes in his homily *Against Those Who Lend at Interest.* And indigent parents might be forced to sell one or more of their children into slavery so that the remainder of the family might escape starvation. Basil vividly portrays one such terrible scene in the homily *I Will Tear Down My Barns.*

Another privilege that was available to Basil as a result of his family's wealth and social status was education. As the son of a noted teacher of rhetoric, Basil received an outstanding education in the finest schools of the day. His initial training in rhetoric was carried out by his father. When Basil was about fourteen, he traveled to Caesarea for formal studies. His father died shortly thereafter, making Basil the heir of a considerable fortune. Basil then proceeded to Constantinople for further studies, and finally to the university at Athens, one of the great centers of higher learning in the ancient world. It was in Athens that he first met a young student named Gregory from Nazianzus, a small village neighboring Caesarea. The two became fast friends, a friendship that was to shape the course of both their lives. According to Gregory, Basil became disillusioned

ratio of slaves to free in the ancient world, M.I. Finley offers anecdotal evidence suggesting that the percentage of slaves in Greece and Italy remained relatively stable at around 30–35% from the 5th century BC through the end of the Roman Republic, and began to decline slowly at some point during the later Roman Empire. See his *Ancient Slavery and Modern Ideology* (New York: Viking Press, 1980), 79–80, at 126 ff.

[7] See Susan Holman, *The Hungry Are Dying* (New York: Oxford University Press, 2001), 40.

with the disputations and intrigues he encountered in Athens, and declared his studies there to be for him an "empty happiness."[8] It is possible to imagine them, like so many students after them, as earnest and restless young men, searching for truth and higher purpose. The two resolved together to pursue the way of "true philosophy,"[9] having only one aim in life: "to be and to be called Christians."[10]

After completing his studies at the university, Basil returned to Caesarea in 356. He took up a position as a teacher of rhetoric, following in his father's footsteps, but he was not to occupy the chair of rhetoric for long. It was during this period that the first great turning in Basil's life took place, one of two profound shifts that would have a decisive impact upon his future life and ministry. Basil later described the alteration in his life's trajectory in this way:

> Much time had I spent in vanity, and had wasted nearly all my youth in the vain labor which I underwent in acquiring the wisdom made foolish by God. Then once upon a time, like a man roused from deep sleep, I turned my eyes to the marvelous light of the truth of the Gospel, and I perceived the uselessness of "the wisdom of the princes of this world, who come to naught."[11] . . . Then I read the Gospel, and I saw there that a great means of reaching perfection was the selling of one's goods, sharing them with the poor, giving up all care for this life, and the refusal to allow the soul to be turned by any sympathy to things of earth.[12]

Several events occurred during this pivotal period in Basil's life. He made the decision to be baptized, an event that in his time was often postponed until late in life in order to avoid the commission of sig-

---

[8]*Panegyric on St Basil* 18, Nicene and Post-Nicene Fathers, ser. 2, vol. 7, p. 401 (henceforth, this series will be cited in the following way: NPNF² 7:401).

[9]Ibid. 19 (401).

[10]Ibid. 21 (402).

[11]1 Cor 2.6.

[12]Ep. 223 *Against Eustathius of Sebasteia* (NPNF² 8:263).

nificant sins after receiving baptismal grace. Basil's baptism makes it clear that he saw this moment as a turning point, a decisive break with his past, a new life. From the passage above, it also appears that Basil chose to sell some portion of the inheritance that fell to him after the death of his father, and distribute the proceeds to the poor, in keeping with the commandment of Jesus, "Sell your possessions and give the money to the poor."[13] Basil's brother, Gregory of Nyssa, writes that Basil "ungrudgingly spent upon the poor his patrimony even before he was a priest, and most of all in the time of the famine, during which he was a ruler of the Church, though still a priest in the rank of presbyters, and afterwards did not hoard even what remained to him."[14]

Basil then left Caesarea to travel throughout Palestine, Syria, and Egypt, visiting many of the experimental monastic colonies that were developing in those regions. These communities, like the first Christian community in Jerusalem, shared a common life of prayer and worship, and held all their goods in common as well, so that no one could properly call anything his or her own. Basil was profoundly impressed by this communal or "cenobitic" way of life. He returned from his travels to the family estate at Annisa, where his mother and sister Macrina had already established a monastic community for women, and settled in a remote, wooded area of the property across the River Iris to live a life of prayer and solitude as an ascetic. He was joined by others of like mind from the surrounding area, and a community soon developed, patterned after the cenobitic way of monastic life Basil had witnessed during his travels. Basil extended an invitation to his friend Gregory, who traveled from Nazianzus to stay at Annisa for a time.

Although Annisa was an isolated and peaceful place, the world outside was in a period of profound social and theological upheaval. Economic factors such as heavy taxation of the lower classes to support the military and the increasing concentration of land in the

---

[13]Mt 19.21.
[14]*Against Eunomius* 1.10 (NPNF[2] 5:45).

hands of wealthy absentee landlords were sharpening the distinctions between rich and poor.[15] At the same time, the resurgence of the Arian heresy in the form of Eunomianism[16] threatened the internal stability of both the Church and the state. Basil's sojourn at Annisa, lasting from about 358 to 364, was not a period of unbroken seclusion. In 359, he traveled to Constantinople with a delegation from Caesarea to participate in a council convened to discuss theological issues surrounding the Arian heresy. What he saw during this and other excursions would have contrasted sharply with the serenity of Annisa: on the one hand, a world being torn apart by seemingly intractable theological divisions; on the other, an unbalanced social structure enriching a few while leaving many without the means to meet their daily needs. Basil seems to have felt a growing sense of responsibility for these problems, and a desire to make some contribution towards the good of the Church and society. And so, some six years after his retirement to Annisa, the second great turning in Basil's life took place: his decision to leave the community at Annisa and return to the world with its divisions and difficulties, bringing with him the fruits of his silence and prayer, his experience of communal monastic life, and his considerable rhetorical and theological acumen. Basil was ordained a priest, and in 365 began parish ministry in Caesarea.

These two turnings—Basil's decision to pursue a monastic vocation and his subsequent decision to leave the monastery and return to the world—may be said to comprise the polarity of his social vision, the axis upon which his worldview turns. Throughout his

[15]The military doubled in size between the second and fourth centuries in order to counter the barbarian invasions. The enormous tax increases that followed forced many small farmers off their land, which was in turn bought up by the wealthier classes. See A.H.M. Jones, *The Later Roman Empire 284–602: A Social Economic and Administrative Survey,* vol. II (Norman, OK: University of Oklahoma Press, 1964), 1035, 1039, 1045–46.

[16]Eunomius was a disciple of Aetius, who taught that the Son's being was "unlike" (ἀνόμοιος) that of the Father; hence the name of their sect, the "Anomoeans." Basil wrote an extensive refutation of Eunomius' teachings, his treatise *Against Eunomius.* See Rousseau, *Basil of Caesarea,* pp. 106–16.

ministry, Basil remained committed to the ideal of a community of shared life and resources, as exemplified by cenobitic monasticism. But he was equally determined that this ideal should not be limited to a monastic context, but should rather be brought to bear upon the larger society. Basil envisioned a new social order based upon simplicity and sharing rather than competition and private ownership. His ideals were quickly put to the test. In 369, within a few years of his ordination to the priesthood, a major catastrophe struck Caesarea and the surrounding area, a drought followed by a severe famine. Rivers and springs dried up and crops failed, resulting in an acute food shortage throughout the region. The four homilies that comprise the bulk of this work appear to have been delivered around the time of the famine. It was at this time that Basil truly "found his voice" with regard to social issues, earning his reputation as one of the most powerful orators in the Christian East on matters of social justice.

Holy Simplicity: Basil as Priest and Homilist

As was noted above, Basil describes his own conversion as having taken place as a result of "reading the Gospel" with regard to "the selling of one's goods" and "sharing them with the poor." In order to gain a better understanding of Basil's approach to matters of wealth and poverty, therefore, it is instructive to begin by examining his exegesis of the account concerning the rich young ruler found in the Synoptic Gospels, and comparing his interpretation with that of some other early Christian exegetes. How to understand Christ's injunction to the young man, "If you wish to be perfect, go, sell your possessions, and give the money to the poor, and you will have treasure in heaven; then come, follow me,"[17] was a subject of considerable discussion in the early Church. One interpretive approach to the passage that proved highly influential in subsequent Christian

[17]Mt 19.21.

thought was proposed in the early third century by St Clement of Alexandria. In his oration *Who Is the Rich Man That Shall Be Saved?* Clement focuses upon the young man's unhealthy attachment to worldly goods. According to Clement, Christ is not asking the young man literally to dispense with his possessions, but rather to become a free person by breaking his attachment to them, since the person who is concerned about acquiring or keeping wealth is not truly free.[18] As Clement says:

> [The saying] is not what some hastily take it to be, a com-
> mand to fling away the substance that belongs to him and
> to part with his riches, but to banish from the soul its
> opinions about riches, its attachments to them, its excessive
> desire, its morbid excitement over them, its anxious cares,
> the thorns of our earthly existence, which choke the seed
> of the true life.[19]

Clement concludes that what Christ intends for the young man is something other than "the outward act which others have done," that the Lord's command rather aims at "the stripping off of the passions from the soul itself and from the disposition, and the cutting up by the roots and casting out of what is alien to the mind."[20]

Soul

In the late third and early fourth centuries, another reading of the commandment came to great prominence in the Church with the rise of the monastic movement. In contrast to Clement's approach, monastic literature of this period tends to emphasize the need to make a decisive break with the world by fully renounc-

---

[18]For a thorough discussion of Clement's approach, see Annewies van den Hoek, "Widening the Eye of the Needle: Wealth and Poverty in the Works of Clement of Alexandria," in *Wealth and Poverty in Early Church and Society,* Susan R. Holman ed. (Grand Rapids, MI: Baker Academic and Brookline, MA: Holy Cross Orthodox Press, 2008), 67–75.

[19]Clement of Alexandria *The Rich Man's Salvation* 11; *Clement of Alexandria,* trans. G.W. Butterworth, Loeb Classical Library 92 (Cambridge, MA.: Harvard University Press, 1919), 290–293.

[20]Ibid., 12.

ing and giving away one's possessions. According to the *Life of St Anthony* written by St Athanasius, this is precisely what St Anthony did after hearing the story of the rich young ruler being read in the church: "Anthony, as though God had put him in mind of the Saints, and the passage had been read on his account, went out immediately from the church, and gave the possessions of his forefathers to the villagers, so that they should no longer be a burden upon himself and his sister."[21] The thrust of the monastic approach, as exemplified by Anthony, is not the aid that is rendered to the poor by giving one's property to them, but rather the need to rid oneself of the burden of worldly possessions. In fact, "the poor" as they are referenced in the monastic writings of this period are nearly always the *anonymous* poor; they remain nameless and faceless, little more than a cipher, a receptacle for discarded possessions.

The tension between these two interpretive constructs—the more figurative approach of Clement vs. the more literal approach of the monastic movement—was eventually resolved to some extent by making a distinction between those who live out their Christian vocation "in the world" vs. those who live as monks and nuns. The former are enjoined not to become overly attached to their material possessions, while the latter fulfill the commandment in its literal sense, which is regarded as the way to true perfection. This "two-tiered" approach to the commandment is eventually codified in the West through the formal distinction between "precepts" (commandments obligatory for everyone) and "counsels" (teachings that are applicable only to those seeking a higher Christian ideal; that is, monastics). In the East this approach is expressed through the notions of "monastic perfection" and the "angelic life."

For all their differences, both of the approaches described above, that of Clement and that of the early monastic movement, are united in addressing the spiritual condition of the young man in almost exclusively individual terms; both understand the root problem as residing in his relationship to wealth and worldly goods per se.

---

[21] Athanasius *Life of Antony* 2 (NPNF[2] 4:196).

When we turn to Basil's interpretation of this passage, therefore, it is highly significant to note that Basil understands the spiritual malady of the rich young ruler not as overattachment to worldly things, but rather as a violation of the commandment, "You shall love your neighbor as yourself." In other words, Basil interprets this story in primarily social rather than individual terms. As he says with regard to the rich young ruler in his homily *To the Rich:*

> It is thus evident that you are far from fulfilling the commandment, and that you bear false witness within your own soul that you have loved your neighbor as yourself. Look, the Lord's offer shows just how distant you are from true love! For if what you say is true, that you have kept from your youth the commandment of love and have given to everyone the same as to yourself, then how did you come by this abundance of wealth? Care for the needy requires the expenditure of wealth: when all share alike, disbursing their possessions among themselves, they each receive a small portion for their individual needs. Thus, those who love their neighbor as themselves possess nothing more than their neighbor; yet surely, you seem to have great possessions! How else can this be, but that you have preferred your own enjoyment to the consolation of the many? For the more you abound in wealth, the more you lack in love.[22]

The commandment to "love your neighbor as yourself," which Basil describes as "the mother of the commandments,"[23] is thus the basis for Basil's understanding of Christ's injunction to the rich young ruler. The focus is not on the individual's relationship to wealth and possessions, but rather on the fact that having great wealth while others lack daily necessities constitutes a violation of the law of love.

[22]Basil *To the Rich* 1.
[23]Basil *In Time of Famine and Drought* 7.

For this reason, Basil explicitly rejects any attempt to formulate a two-tiered approach to the commandment. In Basil's view, "sell your possessions and give to the poor" is an expression of the law of love, and is therefore equally applicable to all, both monastics and non-monastics. As he states in *To the Rich,*

> Was the command found in the Gospel, "If you wish to be perfect, sell your possessions and give the money to the poor," not written for the married? After seeking the blessing of children from the Lord, and being found worthy to become parents, did you at once add the following, "Give me children, that I might disobey your commandments; give me children, that I might not attain the Kingdom of Heaven"?[24]

Moreover, in contrast with the "anonymous poor" found throughout much of the monastic literature, Basil's homilies are characterized by a deliberate attempt to humanize and personalize the plight of the poor. He wonders aloud more than once, "How can I bring the sufferings of the poor to your attention?" Basil brings his powerful gift of rhetoric to bear in order to reveal the face of the neighbor: the emaciated face of the starving person who has gone blind as a result of malnutrition, the agonized face of a parent forced to sell a child into slavery in order to save the rest of the family from starvation. He is determined that the faces of those who suffer should not remain hidden.

---

[24]Basil *To the Rich* 7. Basil also writes in the treatise *On Renunciation of the World,* "Does it not seem to you, then, that the Gospel applies to married persons also? Surely, it has been made clear that obedience to the Gospel is required of all of us, both married and celibate. The man who enters the married state may well be satisfied in obtaining pardon for his incontinency and desire of a wife and marital existence, but the rest of these precepts are obligatory for all alike and are fraught with peril for transgressors." *St Basil: Ascetical Works,* Sr M. Monica Wagner, trans., Fathers of the Church 9 (Washington, DC: Catholic University Press, 1962) 17.

The Ethic of Sustainability

If the commandment to sell one's possessions and give to the poor is an expression of the law of love and thus binding upon all, then the question may well be asked, "How is this commandment to be lived out in practical terms?" We may answer by saying that one of the primary characteristics of the new community envisioned by Basil is what might be called the *ethic of sustainability*. In essence, this means that the law of love requires people to adopt a way of life that is supportable across the entire populace. Basil's social vision is characterized by a commitment to simplicity as a means to ensuring this sustainable way of life for everyone. As noted above, he states that the equitable distribution of resources requires that each person take a "small portion" so that there might be enough for all. Basil emphasizes simplicity in food, dress, and housing as a way of being that allows for resources to be fairly distributed. With regard to housing, he emphasizes that "walls whether great or small serve the same purpose."[25] With reference to interior furnishings he asks the rhetorical question, "What better service do silver encrusted tables and chairs or ivory inlaid beds and couches provide than their simpler counterparts?"[26] And concerning food and clothing he says, "Two lengths of cloth are sufficient for a coat, and a single garment fulfills every need with regard to clothing . . . A loaf of bread is enough to fill your stomach."[27] He harshly criticizes the wealthy of his day for their excessive consumption—sumptuous meals, lavish dress, large and ornately decorated houses—which he sees as directly linked to the plight of the poor. As he says in *To the Rich,* "You gorgeously array your walls, but do not clothe your fellow human being; you adorn horses, but turn away from the shameful plight of your brother or sister; you allow grain to rot in your barns, but do not feed those who are starving; you hide gold in the earth, but ignore the oppressed!"[28]

[25] *To the Rich* 4.
[26] Ibid.
[27] Ibid 2.
[28] Ibid 4.

Basil's ethic of sustainability is based upon an economic philosophy that might be described as a "limited resource paradigm." He believes that God has provided enough food, land, and usable materials to satisfy the needs of all; these resources, however, are limited commodities, and must therefore be shared out equitably. In Basil's view, a healthy economic system requires that resources remain in constant circulation, rather than being stored up or accumulated in large amounts for the benefit of a few individuals. As he writes in his homily *I Will Tear Down My Barns,*

> When riches are closed up like this so that they become stagnant, what do they do for you? . . . Wells become more productive if they are drained completely, while they silt up if they are left idle. Thus wealth left standing is of no use to anyone, but put to use and exchanged it becomes fruitful and beneficial for the public.[29]

When some people use or hoard excessive amounts of resources, there will necessarily be less for others to use. As Basil says in the same homily, "If we all took only what was necessary to satisfy our own needs, giving the rest to those who lack, no one would be rich, no one would be poor, and no one would be in need."[30]

The Distributive Mandate

The corollary to Basil's teaching with regard to the ethic of sustainability is what might be called the "distributive mandate." The content of the distributive mandate is that whatever one has that is "extra," over and above one's actual needs, should be given to those who have less. Basil describes this process with a beautiful Greek word, ἐπανισοῦν, which literally means "to restore the balance," to

---

[29]Basil *I Will Tear Down My Barns* 5.
[30]Basil *I Will Tear Down My Barns* 7.

re-establish equilibrium within an unbalanced situation or equation.[31] The distributive mandate is essentially a responsibility to observe the commandment of love by sharing with others. In one of his most often-quoted passages, Basil says, "The bread you are holding back is for the hungry, the clothes you keep put away are for the naked, the shoes that are rotting away with disuse are for those who have none, the silver you keep buried in the earth is for the needy."[32]

And yet the apparent simplicity of the distributive mandate is complicated by the tendency for people to adjust the definition of "need" to fit their current level of income. Simply put, those who have more tend to use more. Basil treats this subject in some detail in his homily *I Will Tear Down My Barns,* which takes as its point of departure Christ's parable about the foolish rich man who said to himself that he would tear down his barns and build larger ones to store his goods.[33] In Basil's treatment of the passage, "tearing down one's barns" becomes a metaphor for describing an expanding baseline of need. According to Basil, the "barn" represents a definition of need, what a person thinks he or she needs to live. Thus, "tearing down one's barns" means redefining one's "needs" based upon a change in one's circumstances. Basil in effect says that if people never have anything extra to share, this is primarily due to the fact that whenever they find themselves in possession of a surplus, they immediately adjust their definition of need to fit the new situation. While the foolish rich man in the parable only thought to tear down his barns one time, such people are in effect constantly tearing down their barns in order to build larger ones, only to tear these down and build them up again:

[You say], 'I will pull down my barns and build larger ones.' But if you fill these larger ones, what do you intend to do next? Will you tear them down yet again only to build them up once more? What could be more ridiculous than this incessant toil, laboring to build and then laboring to tear down again?[34]

Basil shares with St John Chrysostom the notion that those who possess great resources but refuse to help others are guilty of a kind of theft.[35] "Is not the person who strips another of clothing called a thief?" Basil asks. "And those who do not clothe the naked when they have the power to do so, should they not be called the same?"[36] And yet Basil goes even further than this. According to Basil, those who refuse to share with others in time of urgent need, when starvation and disease pose an imminent threat to human life, may be accounted guilty not only of theft, but even of murder. As he writes in the homily *In Time of Famine and Drought,* delivered at the height of the famine in Caesarea, "Whoever has the ability to remedy the suffering of others, but chooses rather to withhold aid out of selfish motives, may properly be judged the equivalent of a murderer."[37] The sobering thrust of the distributive mandate may thus be summarized in these words from *I Will Tear Down My Barns*: "You are guilty of injustice towards as many as you might have aided, and did not."[38]

It is important to note that Basil is interested not only in ameliorating the plight of the poor, but also in identifying and reforming

[34]Basil *I Will Tear Down My Barns* 6.

[35]" 'See the man,' He says, 'and his works; indeed this also is theft, not to share one's possessions.' Perhaps this statement seems surprising to you, but do not be surprised. I shall bring you testimony from the divine Scriptures saying that not only the theft of others' goods but also the failure to share one's own goods with others is theft and swindle and defraudation." John Chrysostom *Second Sermon on Lazarus and the Rich Man*; in *St John Chrysostom: On Wealth and Poverty,* Catharine P. Roth, trans. (Crestwood, NY: St Vladimir's Seminary Press, 1984), 49.

[36]Basil *I Will Tear Down My Barns* 6.

[37]Basil *In Time of Famine and Drought* 7.

[38]Basil *I Will Tear Down My Barns* 8.

the structures that create and reinforce the cycle of poverty. He is particularly severe in his condemnation of predatory lenders who target the poor, exploiting their vulnerable and insecure position in order to take what little they have. Basil accuses such people of "seeking a harvest from the desert" by "making the hardships of the miserable an occasion for profit."[39] He also says,

> In truth it is the height of inhumanity that those who do not have enough even for basic necessities should be compelled to seek a loan in order to survive, while others, not being satisfied with the return of the principal, should turn the misfortune of the poor to their own advantage and reap a bountiful harvest.[40]

He describes these lenders as predators in the truest sense, "rushing like a hound to the hunt," while the debtors "quail like quarry at the pursuit";[41] he urges the prospective borrower, "do not allow yourself to be tracked and hunted down like some kind of prey."[42] Basil warns the poor to live within their constrained means so as not to become trapped in the downward spiral of debt, vividly describing the miserable life of the debtor who lives in terror of meeting the creditor. But he concludes with stern words for the lenders who oppress them: "Listen, you rich, to the kind of counsel I am giving to the poor on account of your inhumanity: to remain in dreadful circumstances, rather than accepting the assistance offered by loans at interest."[43] He urges these lenders to convert their loans into gifts, entrusting to the poor the portion of their money that lies idle and unused, in confidence that God will serve as guarantor on these "loans," providing a rich return on their investment.

---

[39]Basil *Against Those Who Lend at Interest* 1.
[40]Ibid.
[41]Ibid. 2.
[42]Ibid.
[43]Ibid. 5.

The Conversion to Sociability

Throughout Basil's homilies on social themes, one of the most commonly repeated words is the Greek adjective κοινός, meaning "shared" or "common," a cognate of the word κοινωνία or "communion." Basil uses this word repeatedly to underscore what is for him a basic moral premise: The world was created for the common benefit of all, and given by God to humanity for their shared use. He especially delights in using nature images to illustrate this point; for example, in his homily *In Time of Famine and Drought,* Basil says:

> The animals use in common the plants that grow naturally from the earth. Flocks of sheep graze together upon one and the same hillside, herds of horses feed upon the same plain, and all living creatures permit each other to satisfy their need for food. But we hoard what is common, and keep for ourselves what belongs to many others.[44]

He also speaks of how the earth itself does not discriminate between rich and poor or between owners and non-owners.

> The earth was welcoming all to its richness: it germinated the crops deep in the furrows, produced large clusters of grapes on the vine, made the olive tree bend under a vast quantity of fruit, and offered every delicious variety of the fruit tree. But the rich man was unwelcoming and unfruitful; he did not even possess as yet, and already he begrudged the needy.[45]

As may be noted from these passages, Basil regards the selfishness of human behavior as a kind of anomaly within creation. Although competition within and among species is a normal part of the natural order, only humans compete in such a way as to take more

---

[44]Basil *In Time of Famine and Drought* 8.
[45]Basil *I Will Tear Down My Barns* 5.

than they actually need or can possibly use, while depriving others of what is necessary for their survival. Throughout the homilies, Basil describes the phenomena of human overconsumption and hypercompetition through the categories of disease, compulsion, and addiction. At one point, Basil says that such selfish behaviors can only be attributed to "some device concocted by the devil,"[46] since no rational foundation or basis in actual need can be found for them.

The world was created by God in order to be shared; for this reason, Basil says, private ownership of resources meant to be held in common distorts people's relationships to each other and to the world. Responding to an imaginary interlocutor who has just asked why it is unjust to keep what is "one's own," Basil replies:

> Tell me, what is your own? What did you bring into this life? From where did you receive it? It is as if someone were to take the first seat in the theater, then bar everyone else from attending, so that one person alone enjoys what is offered for the benefit of all in common—this is what the rich do. They seize common goods before others have the opportunity, then claim them as their own by right of preemption.[47]

Basil describes such people, those who live by the rule of competition and private ownership, as ἀκοινώνητοι, meaning "unsocial" or "unsociable." He says of the foolish rich man who tore down his barns that God was "inviting his soul to a more social and civilized demeanor."[48] Similarly, according to Basil, God is calling every person to become a κοινωνικὸς ἄνθρωπος, a "social human being," one who understands his or her social obligations and lives in proper relation to his or her neighbor. Sociability is seen not merely as a virtuous quality, but rather as a conversion to a new way of being in the world. Basil goes so far as to say that sharing has the power

[46]Basil *To the Rich* 2.
[47]Basil *I Will Tear Down My Barns* 7.
[48]Ibid. 1.

to undo the original sin of Adam and Eve. "Give but a little, and you will gain much; undo the primal sin by sharing your food. Just as Adam transmitted sin by eating wrongfully, so we wipe away the treacherous food when we remedy the need and hunger of our brothers and sisters."[49] Thus, one might even say that the conversion to sociability represents the beginning of a new world, a foretaste of the new creation.

THE NEW CITY: BASIL'S EPISCOPAL MINISTRY

In Gregory of Nazianzus' funeral oration for Basil, Gregory describes the practical legacy of Basil's philanthropic endeavors in this way: "Go forth a little way from the city, and behold the new city, the storehouse of piety, the common treasury of the wealthy . . . where disease is regarded in a religious light, and disaster is thought a blessing, and sympathy is put to the test."[50] Gregory is referring to the great philanthropic foundation founded by Basil that later came to be known as the *Basiliad.* Here, the poor and diseased were able to receive food, shelter, and medical treatment free of charge. The *Basiliad* was in many ways the culmination of Basil's social vision, the fruit of his efforts to develop a more just and humane social order within the region of Caesarea. Its presence is eloquent testimony to the fact that Basil was more than a man of words; he was also a man of action.

The early institution of the *Basiliad* seems to have had its roots in Basil's efforts to assist the victims of the drought and famine of 369. During this time, Basil sold and distributed much of what remained of his paternal inheritance in order to help provide for the starving people of Caesarea. By his word and example, he was also able to prevail upon the consciences of many wealthy people to open their storehouses and share with the poor. As Gregory states in the funeral

[49]Basil *Famine and Drought* 7.
[50]Gregory of Nazianzus *Panegyric on St Basil* 63 (NPNF[2] 7:416).

oration, "For by his word and advice he opened the stores of those who possessed them, and so, according to the Scripture, dealt food to the hungry, and satisfied the poor with bread, and fed them in the time of dearth, and filled the hungry souls with good things."[51] In this same oration, Gregory describes Basil as a "second Joseph,"[52] echoing Basil's own injunction during the famine that those who possessed means should "imitate Joseph in his philanthropic proclamation."[53] The *Basiliad* thus appears to have had its origin during Basil's priestly ministry as a distribution center for surplus food and other goods, which were dispensed to the needy under Basil's supervision.

In 370, Basil was elected bishop of Caesarea, a position he was to occupy until his untimely death in 379. The *Basiliad* expanded significantly during Basil's episcopal ministry, partly through the patronage of the Emperor Valens and the support of other benefactors. It eventually grew into a large complex of buildings that not only served as a distribution center for donated goods, but also provided shelter to the homeless and skilled medical services to the sick, especially treatment for leprosy with its associated social stigma. Basil himself was known for his willingness to care for the victims of leprosy personally, thus providing an example for others to follow, as Gregory recounts in his funeral oration:

He did not therefore disdain to honor with his lips this disease, noble and of noble ancestry and brilliant reputation though he was, but saluted them as brethren. . . . The effect produced is to be seen not only in the city, but in the country and beyond, and even the leaders of society have vied with one another in their philanthropy and magnanimity towards them. Others have had their cooks, and splendid tables, and the devices and dainties of confectioners, and exquisite car-

[51]Ibid. 35 (407).
[52]Ibid. 36.
[53]Basil *I Will Tear Down My Barns* 2.

riages, and soft, flowing robes; Basil's care was for the sick, and the relief of their wounds, and the imitation of Christ, by cleansing leprosy, not by a word, but in deed.[54]

The bishop's residence and housing for the clergy and personnel who worked there were also located within the *Basiliad*. Basil's letters give the impression of a bustling center of activity: physicians and nurses, cooks and attendants, clergy and ascetics all working together to minister to the physical and spiritual needs of the sick and destitute.[55]

In addition to being a philanthropic institution, the *Basiliad* was also an important spiritual center, a place of worship and religious education. Basil's letters speak of a chapel within the complex where important religious observances took place,[56] and also describe the *Basiliad* as a place where people came to be instructed in the principles of simplicity and sharing:

According to his custom the very godly bishop [i.e., Basil] visited it [the *Basiliad*], and I consulted him as to the points which you had urged upon me. . . . [He said], "the rule ought to be that every one should limit his possessions to one garment." For one proof of this he quoted the words of John the Baptist "he that hath two coats let him impart to him that hath none;" and for another our Lord's prohibition to His disciples to have two coats. He further added, "If thou wilt be perfect go and sell that thou hast and give to the poor."[57]

---

[54]Gregory of Nazianzus *Panegyric on St Basil* 63 (NPNF² 7:416).

[55]Basil *Epistle* 94 (NPNF² 8:179–180).

[56]Basil *Epistle* 176 (NPNF² 8:220).

[57]Basil *Epistle* 150.3 (NPNF² 8:208). Although Basil himself is the author of this letter, it is written as though it were authored by Heracleidas, a friend of Amphilochius, to whom the letter is addressed; Basil thus speaks of himself obliquely in the third person.

Basil describes this way of life as "the polity that accords with Christ" (ἡ κατὰ Χριστὸν πολιτεῖα).[58] All of this suggests that the *Basiliad* was not merely an institution for helping the poor, but also a worshipping and learning community comprised of people from many different backgrounds committed to a common life of sharing and service. One might even describe it as a kind of "alternative society" with its own economy and polity, a "new city" in the truest sense.

The *Basiliad* was perhaps the highest expression of Basil's attempt to bring the ideals of cenobitic monastic practice, with its emphasis upon shared life and resources, to bear upon the larger society in order to create a new social order. And yet the pressing needs of this society also led Basil progressively to envision a new kind of monasticism: urban rather than rural in character, and dedicated to service to the poor as an essential aspect of monastic practice.[59] This was in many ways a departure not only from the monastic practice he had witnessed in Syria, Palestine, and Egypt, but also from his own earlier practice at Annisa. Basil's vision of an "engaged monasticism" is expressed within the collection of his writings to monastic communities known as the *Great Asceticon,* containing the so-called *Longer Rules* and *Shorter Rules,* as well as various other writings of an ascetic character. According to the *Longer Rules,* monastics were expected to practice a trade such as carpentry, masonry, or blacksmithing; this required that monastic communities be located near cities rather than in remote locations, giving Basil's monastic vision a decidedly urban flavor. Income derived from these occupations was to be used to assist those in need. The *Longer Rules* emphasize the importance of care for the poor by repeatedly referring to Matthew 25:31–46 and Christ's statement "I was hungry and you fed me . . . inasmuch as you did it to the least of these, you did it to me."[60]

---

[58]Basil *Epistle* 150.1 (207). Cf. Rousseau, *Basil of Caesarea,* 144.

[59]For Basil's influence on monastic patterns of philanthropy, cf. Demetrios J. Constantelos, *Byzantine Philanthropy and Social Welfare* (New Brunswick, NJ: Rutgers University Press, 1968), 88–90.

[60]Basil *Longer Rules* 3, 37; Wagner, *Ascetical Works,* 240, 307.

Care for the needy was facilitated through the development of hospices or *xenodocheia,* adjunct institutions located within or adjacent to the monasteries, where the hungry were fed and the sick cared for. As Basil writes in the *Shorter Rules,* "We teach those who minister in the hospice (ἐν τῷ ξενοδοχείῳ) to minister to the sick with such care, as if ministering to the brothers and sisters of Christ. . . . "[61] Basil's treatise *On Renunciation of the World* also contains an important description of such ministry:

> When it is your turn to serve, add to your physical labor a word of exhortation and comfort for love of those whom you serve, that your ministry, seasoned with salt, may be acceptable. . . . Perform the duties of your ministry decently and with care as if serving Christ, for "Cursed," says the Prophet, "be every man that doth the work of the Lord negligently." Fear, as if the eye of the Lord were upon you, the perversity which arises from fastidiousness and contempt, even though the task in hand seems a menial one. The work of the ministry is an exalted work and leads to the Kingdom of Heaven. It is a dragnet of the virtues, comprising within itself all the commandments of God. It contains, first of all, the virtue of virtues, humility, which brings with itself a host of blessings; secondly, there is that saying of the Lord, "I was hungry and you gave me to eat; I was thirsty and you gave me to drink; a stranger and weak and in prison and you ministered to me."[62]

Although the specific context of the service described is not mentioned, the passage seems to refer to ministry in the hospice. Basil describes a regular and rotating service among the monastics in a

---

[61]*Shorter Rules* 155 (PG 31:1184B). Constantelos interprets this mention of the *"xenodocheion"* as referring to the *Basiliad* itself; cf. *Byzantine Philanthropy and Social Welfare,* 155.

[62]Basil *On Renunciation of the World;* Wagner, *Ascetical Works,* 29.

ministry of care for others, following the Lord's command to feed the hungry and care for the sick. One might say that the institution of the hospice occupied a similar position vis-à-vis the monastery as the *Basiliad* did in relation to the city.

In conclusion, it is important to emphasize that the "newness" of Basil's new city is not so much an *institutional* newness as it is an *eschatological* newness. That is, the *Basiliad* is not primarily a new kind of charitable institution, but rather a new set of relationships, a new social order that both anticipates and participates in the creation of "a new heaven and new earth where justice dwells."[63] In the *Basiliad,* people living together in voluntary simplicity and service created a new kind of community with the involuntary poor. There could be no better summation of the characteristics of this new city than Basil's own description of the first church at Jerusalem: "Let us zealously imitate the early Christian community, where everything was held in common—life, soul, concord, a common table, indivisible kinship—while unfeigned love constituted many bodies as one and joined many souls into a single harmonious whole."[64] The new city is present wherever people live together in this way, waiting for the Kingdom of God even as they constitute a sign of its presence in our midst.

THE TEXTS

The present work contains original translations from the Greek of four homilies by Basil, *To the Rich, I Will Tear Down My Barns, In Time of Famine and Drought,* and *Against Those Who Lend at Interest,* as well as one homily attributed to Basil, *On Mercy and Justice,* which has been placed as an appendix with its own introduction. I began work translating these texts on Clean Monday, 2003, out of a desire to provide a collection of English translations in contempo-

[63] 2 Pet 3.13.
[64] Basil *In Time of Famine and Drought* 8.

rary language for texts that either remained untranslated or were scattered throughout various works, some out of print and hard to obtain. *To the Rich* appears here for the first time in a complete English translation. I am a "good-natured debtor" to the previous English translations of *I Will Tear Down My Barns* by M.F. Toal, *In Time of Famine and Drought* by Susan R. Holman, *Against Those Who Lend at Interest* by Sr Agnes Clare Way, and *On Mercy and Justice* by Sr M. Monica Wagner, as well as to the modern Greek translations of the four main homilies by Panagiotis Chrestou, for the opportunity to compare and check my own work.

The present volume represents the first collection of Basil's homilies on themes of social justice in the English language. I have departed somewhat from the traditional ordering of the texts by placing *To the Rich* (Homily 7) first, instead of after *I Will Tear Down My Barns* (Homily 6) and before *In Time of Famine and Drought* (Homily 8). This seems to me a more natural progression. *To the Rich* is primarily a philosophical work that lays the groundwork for Basil's thought on wealth and poverty; it may have been delivered at some time before the famine of 369. There is a heightened sense of urgency in the homily *I Will Tear Down My Barns* that would seem to indicate an actual food shortage, a shortage that becomes even more acute in the homily *In Time of Famine and Drought*. The homily *Against Those Who Lend at Interest* is taken from Basil's homilies on the Psalms, where it is listed as *Homily Two on Psalm 14*, but it is often collected together with these other texts due to the "social" nature of its content.

To the Rich

Then someone came to Jesus and said, "Teacher, what good deed must I do to have eternal life?" And he said to him, "Why do you ask me about what is good? There is only one who is good. If you wish to enter into life, keep the commandments." He said to him, "Which ones?" And Jesus said, "You shall not murder; You shall not commit adultery; You shall not steal; You shall not bear false witness; Honor your father and mother; also, You shall love your neighbor as yourself." The young man said to him, "I have kept all these; what do I still lack?" Jesus said to him, "If you wish to be perfect, go, sell your possessions, and give to the poor, and you will have treasure in heaven; then come, follow me." When the young man heard this word, he went away grieving, for he had many possessions.

Matthew 19.16–22

1 We have spoken previously about this young man, and the attentive listener will surely recall the matters we examined at that time. First, we should remember that the youth of this passage is not the same as the lawyer mentioned in the Gospel of Luke.[1] That lawyer was a tempter who crafted his questions disingenuously. But this young man inquired with a healthy disposition, though he did not readily receive the reply. Indeed, he would not have gone away grieving after hearing the Lord's answer if his questions had merely been a ruse. His behavior thus presents a kind of mixed message: in one way, the Scripture shows the young man to be praiseworthy; in

---

[1] Lk 10.25 ff.

another, however, he is seen as pitiable and completely abject. He recognized the Teacher of Truth, bypassing the imposture of the Pharisees, the speculation of the lawyers, and the convocation of the scribes, and ascribed a fitting appellation to the only true and good teacher—for this he is to be praised. Moreover, he desired to learn by what worthy deed he might inherit eternal life—this also is deserving of acceptance. Yet all his good intent is cast under judgment by this: that he does not focus on what is truly good, but rather looks to what pleases most people. Namely, after learning the lessons of salvation from the true teacher, he neither inscribes them in his heart nor puts them into practice, but rather goes away grieving, darkened by the passion of avarice.

All this clearly demonstrates the discord of his motives and his own internal disagreement. Do you say "teacher," and not carry out the duties of a disciple? Do you call him good, yet decline to accept what he offers? After all, it is evident that he who is good is also the giver of good. You ask about eternal life, yet show yourself completely bound to the enjoyment of this present life. What severe, or burdensome, or excessive word did the teacher give to you? "Sell your possessions and give to the poor." If he had offered you the toil of the farmer, or the perils arising from commerce, or any of the difficulties afflicting those who do business, then perhaps you might have been sad at such a disagreeable command. But when he promises to make you an heir of eternal life by such a smooth road, without pain or exertion, you do not rejoice at the ease of salvation, but rather depart with lamentation and bitterness of soul, invalidating all that you accomplished by your previous labor.

Although you say that you have never murdered, or committed adultery, or stolen, or borne false witness against another, you make all this diligence of no account by not adding what follows,[2] which is the only way you will be able to enter the Kingdom of God. If a physician promised to cure some bodily defect, arising either from birth or as a result of illness, you would not lose heart. But when the

---

[2] That is, "You shall love your neighbor as yourself" (Mt 19.19).

Great Physician of souls and bodies, seeing your deficiency in this vital area, wishes to make you whole, you do not accept the joyful news, but rather turn sad and gloomy.

It is thus evident that you are far from fulfilling the commandment, and that you bear false witness within your own soul that you have loved your neighbor as yourself. Look, the Lord's offer shows just how distant you are from true love! For if what you say is true, that you have kept from your youth the commandment of love and have given to everyone the same as to yourself, then how did you come by this abundance of wealth? Care for the needy requires the expenditure of wealth: when all share alike, disbursing their possessions among themselves, they each receive a small portion for their individual needs. Thus, those who love their neighbor as themselves possess nothing more than their neighbor; yet surely, you seem to have great possessions! How else can this be, but that you have preferred your own enjoyment to the consolation of the many? For the more you abound in wealth, the more you lack in love.

If you had truly loved your neighbor, it would have occurred to you long ago to divest yourself of this wealth. But now your possessions are more a part of you than the members of your own body, and separation from them is as painful as the amputation of one of your limbs. Had you clothed the naked, had you given your bread to the hungry, had your door been open to every stranger, had you been a parent to the orphan, had you made the suffering of every helpless person your own, what money would you have left, the loss of which to grieve? Had you determined long ago to give to those in need, how would it be unbearable now to distribute whatever was left? At festival time, people do not regret parting with what they have at hand in order to gain whatever is necessary for the feast; rather, the cheaper they are able to purchase valuable commodities, the more they rejoice at receiving such a bargain. But you lament at relinquishing gold and silver and property—that is, stones and dust—in order to obtain the blessed life.

2   After all, what is the use of wealth? Do you wish to wrap your-self in fine apparel? Surely two lengths of cloth are sufficient for a coat, while the covering of a single garment fulfills every need with regard to clothing. Or would you spend your wealth on food? A loaf of bread is enough to fill your stomach. Why then do you grieve? Of what have you been deprived? Of the glory that derives from wealth? Had you not sought glory from the dirt, you would have discovered the true glory like a shining beacon leading you to the Kingdom of Heaven. Nonetheless, having wealth is dear to you, though you gain from it no advantage whatsoever. And the futility of chasing after what is worthless is obvious to everyone.

Perhaps the lesson of the paradox I am about to speak will be apparent to you; it is, in any case, entirely true. When wealth is scat-tered in the manner which our Lord directed, it naturally returns, but when it is gathered, it naturally disperses. If you try to keep it, you will not have it; if you scatter it, you will not lose it. "They have distributed freely, they have given to the poor; their righteousness endures forever."[3] Yet it is not on account of food or clothing that wealth is sought by most. Rather, some device has been concocted by the devil, suggesting innumerable spending opportunities to the wealthy, so that they pursue unnecessary and worthless things as if they were indispensable, and no amount is sufficient for the expendi-tures they contrive. They divide up their wealth, one part for present needs, and another for the future. They put aside one portion for themselves, and another for their children. Then they distribute their own share among various spending opportunities.

Only listen to the arrangements they make: "There should be," they say, "some wealth for spending, and some held in reserve, while the allowance for daily provisions should exceed the level of mere necessities. Some will be for comforts within the house, and some for outward display; some to make traveling comfortable, and some to make life splendid and luxurious at home." I am overwhelmed even at the thought of so many contrived extravagances! There are

[3]Ps 112.9.

thousands of carriages, plated with bronze and silver; some carry their owners, while others carry their goods. Multitudes of horses follow, whose lineage can be traced back to noble sires, as if they were human beings. Some bear their masters within the city when they go out for entertainment, some are reserved for hunting, while others are specially groomed for traveling. They wear bridles and belts and garlands all of silver and spangled with gold; they are adorned with blankets of finest purple, arrayed like a bridegroom. Teams of mules, separated according to color, are accompanied by their drivers in successive waves, some going before, others following after. A veritable army of servants is required: butlers, housekeepers, gardeners, master artisans of all kinds, experts at both things needful and those devised purely for pleasure and entertainment: cooks, bakers, wine tasters, hunters, sculptors, painters, specialists in every kind of indulgence. There are caravans of camels, some bearing burdens, others grazing. There are teams of horses, droves of cattle, flocks of sheep, herds of swine with their herdsmen. There are landholdings sufficient to pasture them all, while at the same time increasing the sum of wealth by the revenue they generate. The landowners enjoy baths in the city and in the countryside. Their houses are made with all kinds of translucent marble, some of Phrygian stone, some of Lacaonian or Thessalian tile, which keep them warm in the winter and pleasantly cool in the summer. The floors are decorated with mosaic, the ceilings richly gilt. The portions of the walls that are not tiled are decorated with painted designs.

3 After they have squandered their wealth among so many pursuits, if there is any left over, they hide it in the ground and guard it deep within the earth. "For the future," they say, "is always uncertain; therefore let us take care, lest some unforeseen need should arise." Yet while it is uncertain whether you will have need of this buried gold, the losses you incur from your inhuman behavior are not at all uncertain. When by a multitude of schemes you were unable to exhaust your wealth, you concealed it in the earth. An evident madness! So long as gold remained unearthed in the mines, you scoured the world to find it; but once it came to light, you hid it in the earth again. And I think that when it comes to this, as you are burying your wealth, you entomb with it your own heart. "For where your treasure is, there your heart will be also."[4]

This is why the Lord's commands make some sorrowful: because their lives become unbearable when they are not permitted to indulge in frivolous expenditures. It seems to me that the passion of the young man described in the Gospel, and of those like him, may be likened to that of a traveler who hastens to arrive at a famous city, but then stops short and lodges in one of the inns just outside the city walls. By a small degree of laxity, he invalidates all his previous efforts, and deprives himself of beholding the sights of the city. In the same way, there are those who gladly undertake other tasks, but resist laying aside their possessions. I know many who fast, pray, sigh, and demonstrate every manner of piety, so long as it costs them nothing, yet would not part with a penny to help those in distress. Of what profit to them is the remainder of their virtue? The Kingdom of Heaven does not receive such people, for "it is easier for a camel to go through the eye of a needle than for someone who is rich to enter the Kingdom of God."[5]

Although the meaning of our Lord's answer is clear, and he does not lie when he speaks, there are few who are persuaded by it. "How shall we live," someone will say, "when we have renounced everything? What quality of life will there be if everyone sells all and forsakes all?" Do not ask me the rationale behind our Lord's commands. The Lawgiver knows well how to bring what is possible into agreement with the Law. Your heart is tested, as it were, upon the fulcrum of the scale, inclining now towards the true life, now towards present enjoyment. It befits those who possess sound judgment to recognize that they have received wealth as a stewardship, and not for their own enjoyment; thus, when they are parted from it,

[4]Mt 6.21.
[5]Mt 19.24.

they rejoice as those who relinquish what is not really theirs, instead of becoming downcast like those who are stripped of their own.

Why then are you sad? Why do you mourn in your soul, hearing "Sell your possessions"? Even if your belongings could follow you to the future life, they would not be particularly desirable there, since they would be overshadowed by truly precious things. If, on the other hand, they must remain here, why not sell them now and obtain the profit? You are not disappointed when you must spend gold in order to purchase a horse. But when you have the opportunity to exchange corruptible things for the Kingdom of Heaven, you shed tears, spurning the one who asks of you and refusing to give anything, while contriving a million excuses for your own expenditures.

4 What then will you answer the Judge? You gorgeously array your walls, but do not clothe your fellow human being; you adorn horses, but turn away from the shameful plight of your brother or sister; you allow grain to rot in your barns, but do not feed those who are starving; you hide gold in the earth, but ignore the oppressed! And if your wife happens to be a money-loving person, then the disease is doubled in its effects. She stirs up the love of luxury and inflames the craving for pleasure, spurring on fruitless pursuits. Such women contrive to procure precious stones and metals of all kinds—pearls, emeralds, sapphires, and gold—working some into ornaments and weaving some into their garments, while aggravating the disease of avarice with every form of tasteless display. The diligence they bestow on these things is unrivaled; they occupy themselves with such concerns day and night. Multitudes of flatterers insinuate themselves into the household through their desires; they in turn bring in the dye-merchants, the goldsmiths, the perfumers, the weavers, the embroiderers. They do not give anyone a second to breathe with their incessant demands! No amount of wealth, not though rivers should run with gold, can support the desires of a woman who buys imported perfume as though it were common olive oil from the marketplace, and chooses porphyry and sea silk,[6] the flowers of the ocean, over ordinary wool from sheep. Gold settings clasp the costliest of gems; some they make into frontlets for their foreheads and some into necklaces; they weave some into belts, while still more encircles their hands and feet. Indeed, those who love gold do not mind being bound with manacles, so long as their chains are of gold.

How can anyone care for the soul, while catering to the whims of a greedy wife? For as storms and surges at sea scuttle ships with rotten hulls, so the evil disposition of spouses drowns the weaker souls that live with them. When wealth is divided by a man and a woman between so many pursuits, and each vies to outdo the other in the invention of frivolous amusements, there is of course no opportunity to consider the needs of others. When you hear, "Sell what you have and give to the poor," so as to make provision for eternal enjoyment, you go away sad; but when you hear, "give what you have to a woman of luxury"—that is, to stonecutters, woodworkers, mosaicists, painters—you rejoice as though gaining for yourself something money cannot buy.

Do you not see the timeworn remnants of walls that dot the city like so many watchtowers? How many poor people were there in the city, who were ignored by the rich of that day on account of their efforts to construct these walls? Where now is the pristine condition of their works? Where now the one who zealously labored for their grandeur? Are they not razed and utterly demolished, like sand castles designed by children at play? Does not their builder rue in Hades the care taken for spurious things? Let your soul be great; walls whether great or small serve the same purpose. When I go into the house of one of these tasteless newly rich individuals, and see it bedecked with every imaginable hue, I know that this person pos-

---

[6]Porphyry comes from the murex, a mollusk that yields this purple dye highly prized in the ancient world, and associated with nobility: the robes of senators were fringed with purple. Pinna nobilis is another member of the mollusk family that produces fibers of a golden color that are woven into byssus or "sea silk," a very soft and luxurious fabric.

sesses nothing more valuable than what is on display; such people decorate inanimate objects, but fail to beautify the soul.

Tell me, what better service do silver-encrusted tables and chairs or ivory-inlaid beds and couches provide than their simpler counterparts? Yet for their sake the rich do not respond to the poor, not though thousands should come to their door crying with piteous voices. Indeed, you refuse to give anything, insisting that it is impossible to satisfy the needs of those who beg of you. You profess this to be true with your tongue, but your hand gives you the lie; silently, your hand bears witness to the falsehood, flashing as it does with the jewels from your ring. How many could you have delivered from want with but a single ring from your finger? How many households fallen into destitution might you have raised? In just one of your closets there are enough clothes to cover an entire town shivering with cold. You showed no mercy; it will not be shown to you. You opened not your house; you will be expelled from the Kingdom. You gave not your bread; you will not receive eternal life.

5   But you claim that you are yourself a pauper, and I concur. Now a pauper is someone who lacks many things, and the insatiability of your desire makes you lack many things indeed. You diligently strive to add ten more talents to the ten you received, and when you have twenty, you seek to add twenty more. Yet this constant accumulation does not quell the craving, but only further inflames your appetite. For just as a little wine becomes an opportunity for the drunkard to drink some more, so also the newly rich, after they have acquired much, desire even more. They nourish their malady by constant accumulation, and their pursuit of gain is turned against them to their hurt. They do not rejoice in what they have, no matter how much it is, so much as they lament what they still lack, or think they lack. Their soul is eaten away with cares as they compete in the struggle for success. They have every reason to be happy and rejoice in their prosperity, but instead they weep and wail because they fall one or two degrees short of some other super-wealthy individual.

When they surpass one person's fortune, they immediately endeavor to outdo the next wealthier rival, and if they overtake that person, they turn their attention to the next. Like those who ascend a ladder, climbing from rung to rung without stopping until they reach the top, such people do not pause in their race for supremacy until, at the moment they reach the summit, they plunge down headlong from their exalted position.

For the benefit of humanity, the Creator of all things made the starling to devour locusts insatiably; you, on the other hand, have made your own soul insatiable, to the detriment of many. A greedy person desires whatever the eye can take in. "The eye is not satisfied with seeing,"[7] and those who love money will never be satisfied with what they have. Hades never says "enough,"[8] nor does the greedy person ever say "enough." When will you use the things you already have? When will you ever be able to enjoy them, since you suffer constantly from the pains of acquisition?

"Woe to those who join house to house and connect field to field, so that they might rob their neighbor."[9] And what do you do? Do you not contrive a plethora of excuses so as to take what belongs to your neighbor? Someone says, "My neighbors' house blocks the sun," or "they cause disturbances," or "they keep bad company," or makes some other allegation. Such a person never stops badgering and assailing and accusing and harassing until the neighbors are compelled to move elsewhere. What killed Naboth the Israelite? Was it not King Ahab's desire for his vineyard? Truly, the avaricious person is a bad neighbor in both the city and the country. The sea knows its boundaries, the night does not exceed the limits set from of old, but the avaricious person does not regard the passage of time, does not respect any limit, does not defer to the proper order of things, but rather imitates the violent nature of fire: spreading to all and devouring all.

[7] Eccl 1.8.
[8] Cf. Prov 30.16.
[9] Is 5.8 LXX.

Great rivers begin from tiny streams, but eventually acquire irresistible magnitude by means of small additions, so that they violently sweep away whatever lies in their path: thus it is with those who advance to positions of great power. From those who previously held dominance, they receive the ability to treat many others unjustly. They oppress those who remain unscathed through those who are already victims of injustice; as wickedness overflows, it gives them an opportunity to expand their power. Those who have already been badly mistreated render them a kind of involuntary assistance by inflicting harm and injustice upon others in turn.

What neighbor, what confidant, what friend is not swept away? Nothing withstands the influence of wealth. Everything submits to its tyranny, everything cowers at its dominion. Those who have already been exploited would rather avoid suffering some further injury than seek reparations for past injustices. Leading yokes of oxen, the wicked plow, sow, and harvest what is not their own. If you dispute with them, they come to blows with you; if you complain, they accuse you of assaulting them. You will be arrested and put in prison; the false accusers are ever ready, willing to place your very life at risk. Then you will gladly pay something over and above what was already taken in order to settle the matter.

6   It was my intention to give you a respite from the works of injustice and to grant some leisure to your thoughts, so that you might carefully consider to what end your pursuit of material things has led you. You have acres and acres of arable land: fields and orchards, mountains and dells, rivers and springs. But what comes after this? Is not all that awaits you a six-foot plot of earth? Does not a small quantity of rocks and soil suffice to cover this mortal flesh? Why then do you toil? Why do you transgress? Why do you gather a fruitless harvest with your own hands? Would that your labors were only fruitless, and did not rather constitute fuel for the eternal fire!

Will you never rouse yourself from this stupor? Will you never regain consciousness? Will you never come to your senses? Will you not bring before your eyes the Judgment Seat of Christ? What will you say in your own defense, when all around you stand those whom you have treated unjustly, denouncing you before the righteous Judge? What then will you do? What advocates will you retain? What witnesses will you present? How will you sway the Judge who cannot be deceived? No fine speakers are there to defend you, no persuasiveness of speech to hoodwink the Judge. Neither flatterers, nor possessions, nor the burden of glory will follow you there. Without friends, without helpers, without supporters, without even a word in your own defense, you will be led forth in disgrace, with bowed head and downcast eyes, utterly forsaken and ashamed.

Wherever you turn your gaze, you will clearly behold the apparitions of your evil acts: here the tears of the orphan, there the groaning of the widow, elsewhere the poor whom you have trampled down, the servants whom you have brutalized, the neighbors whom you have treated outrageously. All your deeds will rise up before you; the wicked chorus of your wrongdoings will beset you on all sides. Just as the shadow follows the body, so also one's sins closely follow the soul, and form a clear outline of one's actions. There is thus no possibility of denial there; every mouth will be stopped, and especially that of the arrogant. Each person's works will bear witness for themselves; without a word being spoken, they will make our deeds plain. How can I summon before your eyes the fearful things that await you? If indeed you hear and relent of your ways, then remember those days in which "the wrath of God is revealed from heaven."[10] Remember the glorious second coming of Christ, when all will rise, "those who have done good, to the resurrection of life, and those who have done evil, to the resurrection of condemnation."[11] Then everlasting shame will be the portion of sinners, and "a fury of fire that will consume the adversaries."[12] Let all these things make you sad, and not the command of our Lord. How shall I move you? What shall I say? Do you

[10]Rom 1.18.
[11]Jn 5.29.
[12]Heb 10.27.

not desire the Kingdom? Do you not fear hell? Where will healing be found for your soul? If these fearful visages do not move you, if these dazzling images do not compel you, then surely we are dealing with a heart of stone.

7   Consider carefully, you mortal, the true nature of wealth. Why do you find gold so alluring? Gold is, after all, merely a kind of mineral, as is silver or pearl. Chrysolite, beryl, agate, hyacinth, amethyst and jasper: they are all nothing but stones. These indeed comprise the rainbow hues of wealth. Some you hoard for yourself, concealing them and covering their luminous facets with darkness, while the more precious ones you carry with you, filled with conceit by the sight of their luster. Tell me, what benefit do you acquire by waving your hand about resplendent with gems? Should you not rather blush for shame, having this strange desire for pebbles, like the cravings of pregnant women? Expectant mothers sometimes gnaw pebbles, and you have a similarly greedy appetite for brightly colored stones: sardonyx, jasper, and amethyst.

What well-dressed person has ever been granted even one additional day of life? Has death ever spared anyone on account of wealth? Has sickness departed from anyone on account of possessions? How long shall gold be the oppression of souls, the hook of death, the lure of sin? How long shall wealth be the cause of war, for which purpose weapons are forged and sword blades whetted? Because of wealth, kinsfolk disregard the bond of nature, and sibling contemplates murder against sibling. Because of wealth, the desert teems with murderers, the sea with pirates, and the cities with extortionists. Who is the father of lies? Who is the author of forgery? Who gave birth to perjury? Is it not wealth? Is it not the pursuit of wealth? What ails you, people? Who twisted the things that are yours into a plot against you? Material things exist to assist with life; surely they were not given as a provision for wickedness? They constitute a ransom for the soul; surely they were not provided as an occasion for your own destruction?

"But wealth is necessary for rearing children," someone will say. This is a specious excuse for greed; although you speak as though children were your concern, you betray the inclinations of your own heart. Do not impute guilt to the guiltless! They have their own Master who cares for their needs. They received their being from God, and God will provide what they need to live. Was the command found in the Gospel, "If you wish to be perfect, sell your possessions and give the money to the poor," not written for the married? After seeking the blessing of children from the Lord, and being found worthy to become parents, did you at once add the following, "Give me children, that I might disobey your commandments; give me children, that I might not attain the Kingdom of Heaven"?

Who will vouch for the prudence of your children, that they will use what is left to them for good ends? For many, wealth becomes an aid to immorality. Or do you not hear what is said in Ecclesiastes, "There is a grievous ill that I have seen under the sun: riches were kept by their owners to their hurt,"[13] and moreover, "I will leave that for which I have toiled to those who come after me, and who knows whether they will be wise or foolish?"[14] Take care then, lest after countless efforts to acquire riches, you end up providing others with resources to commit sins. In that case, you will find yourself doubly punished, both for acting unjustly in your own right, and for furnishing others with the opportunity to do the same.

Is not your own soul more intimately related to you than any child? Is not its presence the most familiar of all? Give to your soul first in the order of inheritance. Bestow upon it rich provisions for life, and then divide your living amongst your children. Those children who do not receive an inheritance frequently do very well for themselves, but if you leave your own soul an orphan, who will take pity on it?

---

[13]Eccl 5.13.
[14]Eccl 2.18 LXX.

8   The foregoing admonitions were given to parents, but what fine-sounding excuse for miserliness will those who have no children produce for themselves? "I do not sell what I have, nor do I give to the poor, because I need what I have to live." Thus, the Lord is not your teacher, nor does the Gospel govern your life, but you are a lawgiver unto yourself. See what peril you fall into by thinking this way! If the Lord laid these things down as obligatory, but you write them off as unnecessary, it can only mean that you account yourself wiser than the Lawgiver.

Yet you say, "I will enjoy all these things during my life, but after my death I will leave my goods to the poor, making them beneficiaries of my will and granting them all my possessions." When you are no longer among your fellow human beings, then you will become a philanthropist! When I see you dead, then I will call you a lover of your brothers and sisters! You deserve great thanks for your magnanimity, since you became so generous and noble-hearted after you were laid in the grave and your body had dissolved in the earth. Tell me, however, from what period you intend to seek your reward: the time of your life, or that which comes after your departure? When you were still alive, squandering your years in luxury and wasting them on frivolous pursuits, you never bothered to consider the plight of the needy. What exchange is possible now that you are dead? What reward of your labor is due to you? Show your works and seek your recompense. No one transacts business after the end of the festival, nor is anyone who arrives after the close of the games crowned, nor does anyone who comes after the war perform deeds of valor. It is thus apparent that no one can perform good works after the conclusion of this life.

You promise your generosity with mere ink and letters. But who can foretell the time of your departure? Who can be sure of the manner of your end? How many are snatched away by sudden accidents without even having the opportunity to cry out? How many become delirious on account of fever? Why then do you wait for a time when it is likely that you will not even be master of your own thoughts? Dark is the night, and grave the disease, and help nowhere to be found. Those who seek the inheritance are prepared to twist everything to their own advantage and nullify your wishes. Then, when you look around and realize that you are completely forsaken, you will recognize your senselessness and lament your folly. Will you indeed give the order at that moment, when your tongue goes slack in your mouth and your hand trembles uncontrollably, so that neither by spoken nor by written words can you communicate your intent? Even if everything has been clearly spelled out, even if every word has been explicitly declared, one inserted letter is enough to alter your intention completely. One forged seal, two or three false witnesses, and the entire inheritance falls into the hands of others.

9   Why then do you deceive yourself? You wickedly dispose of your wealth now for selfish gratification, while making promises for the future concerning things of which you will no longer be master. As the Word says, your intent is evil:[15] "While I am alive, I will revel in self-indulgence, but when I die, then I will begin practicing the commandments." Abraham will say to you, "During your lifetime you received your good things."[16] You cannot enter by the narrow and difficult way,[17] because you have not shed the burden of wealth. You carried it until the end, instead of laying it aside as you were instructed. While you lived, you put yourself before the commandment, but after death and dissolution, you honor the commandment to spite your enemies: "Let the Lord take what remains, in order that so-and-so may not receive it." What indeed shall we call this: love for your neighbor or revenge upon your enemies?

Read your own will: "I wish that I could have gone on living and enjoying my own things, but . . . " Thus, the gratitude is due to death, not to you. If you were immortal, you would never have remembered

[15]Cf. Ezek 11.2.
[16]Lk 16.25.
[17]Cf. Mt 7.14.

the commandments. "Do not be deceived; God is not mocked."[18] Dead offerings are not accepted at the altar; you must rather present a living sacrifice. The one who makes an offering from remnants will not be accepted. Yet you offer to the Benefactor whatever is left at the end of your life. If you would not dare to entertain dignitaries with the leftovers from your table, how dare you propitiate God with scraps? You rich, behold the final end of avarice, and break your passionate attachment to possessions. The more wealth-loving you are, the more you will take care that none of your goods is lost. Make everything truly your own; transfer everything to the eternal realm; leave none of your wealth behind for strangers!

Perhaps the servants will not even dress you in burial finery at the last, but will desert the graveside, having already transferred their allegiance to the heirs. Perhaps they will even turn philosophical on you: "It is not right," they will say, "to adorn a dead body, and to give a lavish burial to someone who no longer feels anything. Would it not be better to dress the survivors in this elegant and beautiful clothing, rather than allowing such precious garments to rot together with the corpse? What need is there of an officious headstone and a lavish burial, expenses that cannot be recovered? These funds should rather be used by those who remain for their own needs." These things they will say, at once avenging themselves upon you for your tyranny, and ingratiating themselves with those who succeed to your fortune.

In anticipation, therefore, prepare yourself for your own burial. Works of piety are an excellent burial garment. Make your departure dressed in the full regalia of your good deeds; convert your wealth into a truly inseparable adornment; keep everything with you when you go! Be persuaded to this by Christ, the Good Counselor who loves you. He became poor for us so that He might make us rich through His poverty,[19] and "gave Himself a ransom for all."[20] Let

[18]Gal 6.7.
[19]Cf. 2 Cor 8.9.
[20]I Tim 2.6.

us either be persuaded by Him, because He is wise and knows all things, or let us wait patiently for Him, because He loves us, or let us give to Him in return, because He is our Benefactor. In any case, let us do what we have been commanded, that we may become heirs of eternal life in Christ Himself, to whom is due glory and dominion forever and ever. Amen.

I Will Tear Down My Barns

*The land of a rich man produced abundantly. And he thought
to himself, "What should I do, for I have no place to store my
crops?" Then he said, "I will do this: I will pull down my barns
and build larger ones, and there I will store all my grain and
my goods. And I will say to my soul, "Soul, you have ample
goods laid up for many years; relax, eat, drink, be merry." But
God said to him, "You fool! This very night your life is being
demanded of you. And the things you have prepared, whose
will they be?" So it is with those who store up treasures for
themselves but are not rich toward God.*

Luke 12.16–21

1 Temptations come in two forms. Sometimes affliction proves the
heart like gold in a furnace, testing its purity by means of suffering.
But for many, it is prosperity of life that constitutes the greatest trial.
For it is equally difficult to preserve one's soul from despair in hard
times, and to prevent it from becoming arrogant in prosperous circumstances. The great Job, that invincible athlete, is an example of
perseverance in the first kind of temptation. With a steadfast heart
and an unwavering mind, he braved all the devil's violence as if it
were a raging current. The more daunting and formidable the tactics
employed against him by the adversary, the more Job's superiority
over the temptations was clearly demonstrated. But there are others
who are examples of the temptations that come from the good life,
including the rich man whose story was just read for us. Not only did
he possess wealth, but he hoped to obtain even more. As the lover

of humankind, God did not immediately judge him for the ingratitude of his ways, but rather attempted to satisfy him by adding even
more wealth to what he already had, thus inviting his soul to a more
sociable and civilized demeanor.

"The land of a rich man produced abundantly. And he thought
to himself, 'What should I do, for I have no place to store my crops?'
Then he said, 'I will do this: I will pull down my barns and build larger
ones.'"[1] Why did the land produce abundantly, when its owner had
no intention of benefiting others with the abundance? So that the
patience of God might be made manifest, since God's goodness extends
even to people such as this. "For He sends rain on the righteous and
on the unrighteous, and makes His sun rise on the evil and on the
good."[2] Indeed, such goodness on God's part actually serves to heap
even more punishment upon those who do evil. God brought showers
upon the earth that had been cultivated by this man's greedy hands,
and gave sunshine to gently warm the seeds and multiply their produce in abundance. From God comes everything beneficial: fertile soil,
temperate weather, plenty of seeds, cooperation of the animals, and
whatever else is required for successful cultivation. But human beings
respond with a bitter disposition, misanthropy, and an unwillingness
to share. Such characteristics are what this man offered back to his
Benefactor. He did not remember that he shared with others a common
nature, nor did he think it necessary to distribute from his abundance
to those in need. He did not keep even a word of the commandments:
"Do not neglect to do good for the needy,"[3] and "Do not let mercy and
loyalty forsake you,"[4] and "Share your bread with the hungry."[5] He did
not heed the urgings of all the prophets and teachers.

Though his barns were filled to bursting with the abundance
of his goods, his miserly heart was still not satisfied. By constantly
adding more to what he already possessed, augmenting the existing

[1]Lk 12.16–17.
[2]Cf. Mt 5.45; Basil reverses the usual order.
[3]Prov 3.27 LXX.
[4]Prov 3.3 LXX.
[5]Is 58.7.

surplus with annual increases, he fell into this intractable dilemma. He refused to be satisfied with what he already had on account of his greed, yet neither could he store the new harvest on account of its abundance. His purposes thus reached an impasse, and he was at a loss how to proceed. "What should I do?" he wondered. Who would not have pity on someone so besieged with troubles? He was made miserable by abundance, wretched by the good things he possessed, and still more wretched by the good things he still expected to receive. The land does not produce revenue for him, but rather brings forth sighs of discontent; he does not harvest an abundance of produce, but rather cares and sorrows and severe hardship. He laments like those afflicted with poverty. Or rather, do even those hard pressed by poverty give forth such piteous cries? "What should I do? What will I eat? What will I wear?" These things the rich man also exclaims. He is sorely afflicted; his heart is eaten away with cares. What would cause others to rejoice causes the greedy person to waste away. He does not rejoice at all the good things he has in store, but is rather pricked to the heart by the wealth that slips through his fingers, lest perhaps, as it overflows the storehouses, some of it should trickle down to those outside his walls, so as to become a source of aid for those in need.

2   It seems to me that the passion afflicting this man's soul resembles that of the gluttonous, who would rather burst as a result of over-indulgence than share part of what they have with those in need. O mortal, recognize your Benefactor! Consider yourself, who you are, what resources have been entrusted to you, from whom you received them, and why you received more than others. You have been made a minister of God's goodness, a steward of your fellow servants. Do not suppose that all this was furnished for your own gullet! Resolve to treat the things in your possession as belonging to others. After all, they bring pleasure for only a little while, then fade away and disappear, but afterwards a strict accounting of their disbursement will be demanded from you.

But you! You keep everything locked up and securely fastened with gates and bars. You lie awake at night with worry, taking counsel with yourself (and having recourse to a most foolish counselor at that!). "What should I do?" How easily you might have said, "I will satisfy the souls of the hungry, I will throw open the gates of my barns and summon all those in need. I will imitate Joseph in his philanthropic proclamation; I will cry with generous voice: 'Come to me, all you who lack bread, let everyone share as if from common springs in what God has graciously given.'"[6] But you are not such a person. How do I know this? You begrudge your fellow human beings what you yourself enjoy; taking wicked counsel in your soul, you consider not how you might distribute to others according to their needs, but rather how, after having received so many good things, you might rob others of their benefit.

Those who seek the soul were at hand, and this man was conversing with his soul about food! That very night his own soul would be required of him, and all the while he was imagining he would be enjoying his possessions for years to come. He was permitted to make all these decisions and to clearly express his intention, so that he might receive a sentence worthy of his choice.

3   Do not suffer the same thing yourselves. Indeed, it was for this purpose that these things were written, so that we might avoid a similar fate. Imitate the earth, O mortal. Bear fruit as it does; do not show yourself inferior to inanimate soil. After all, the earth does not nurture fruit for its own enjoyment, but for your benefit. But whatever fruit of good works you bring forth, you produce for yourself, since the grace of good works redounds to those who perform them. You gave to the poor, and in so doing not only did you make what you gave truly your own, but you received back even more. For just as grain, when it falls upon the ground, brings forth an increase for the one who scatters it, thus also bread cast to the hungry yields considerable profit at a later time. Therefore, let the end of your

[6]Cf. Gen 41.53–57.

harvesting be the beginning of a heavenly sowing. As the Scripture says, "Sow for yourselves righteousness."[7]

Why then do you go to so much trouble, why do you wear yourself out, seeking to secure your wealth with bricks and mortar? After all, "a good name is to be chosen rather than great riches."[8] If it is the honor that derives from wealth that attracts you, just think how much more glory you will gain by having a multitude of children call you "father" than by having a multitude of gold coins jingling in your purse.[9] You must leave your money behind in the end whether you will or no, but the honor that proceeds from good works will escort you to the Master. All the people will surround you when you stand before the Judge of all, calling you "father" and "benefactor" and all the other titles that pertain to those who show philanthropy. Do you not see those in the theaters, who, for the sake of momentary glory and the applause and acclaim of the crowds, scatter their wealth to wrestlers, actors, animal tamers and the like, even though they are reprehensible characters? And you, are you fainthearted in your spending, when you are about to attain such great glory? God will receive you, angels will extol you, all people from the creation of the world will bless you. Your glory will be eternal; you will inherit the crown of righteousness and the Kingdom of Heaven. All these things will be your reward for your stewardship of perishable things. But you do not even consider them, forgetting about things hoped for in your concern for the things of the present.

Come now, distribute your wealth lavishly, becoming honorable and glorious in your expenditures for the needy. Let what is said of the righteous be said also of you, "They have distributed freely, they have given to the poor; their righteousness endures forever."[10] Do not enhance your own worth by trafficking in the needs of others. Do not wait for a dearth of grain to open your granary: "The people

[7]Hos 10.12.
[8]Prov 22.1.
[9]Basil here seems to play on the assonance between *pater* ("father") and *stater* (a gold coin).
[10]Ps 112.9.

curse those who hold back grain."[11] Do not wait for a famine in order to acquire gold. Do not make common need a means of private gain. Do not become a dealer in human misery. Do not attempt to turn the chastisement of God into an opportunity for profit. Do not chafe the wounds of those who have already been scourged.

You, however, have regard for gold, but not for your own brothers and sisters. You recognize the inscription on the face of a coin, and can tell the counterfeit from the genuine, but you completely ignore your brothers and sisters in their time of need.

4 Yes, while the glitter of gold so allures you, you fail to notice how great are the groans of the needy that follow you wherever you go. How can I bring the sufferings of the poverty-stricken to your attention? When they look around inside their hovels, they do not spy any gold among their things, nor shall they ever. They find only clothes and furnishings so miserable that, if all their belongings were reckoned together, they would be worth only a few cents. What then? They turn their gaze to their own children, thinking that perhaps by bringing them to the slave-market they might find some respite from death. Consider now the violent struggle that takes place between the desperation arising from famine and a parent's fundamental instincts. Starvation on the one side threatens a horrible death, while nature resists, convincing the parents rather to die with their children. Time and again they vacillate, but in the end they succumb, driven by want and cruel necessity.

And what does a parent think at such times? "Which one should I sell first? Which one will earn the greatest favor with the grain merchant? Should I choose the eldest? But I cannot bear to do so, since he is the firstborn. The youngest? But I take pity on his youth, as yet untouched by tragedy. This one looks just like his mother, that one shows aptitude in his lessons. Curse this helplessness! What am I to do? Which of my children shall I strike? What kind of beast shall I become? How can I forget the bond of nature? If I hold onto all of

[11]Prov 11.26.

them, I must watch them all perish with hunger. If I send one of them away, how will I be able to look the others in the eye ever again? They will always view me with suspicion and mistrust. How can I manage my household, when I am responsible for the loss of one of my own children? How can I ever sit down at the table, which now has plenty of food as a result of such a decision?"

And while the parents come with tears streaming down their faces to sell the dearest of their children, you are not swayed by their sufferings; you take no account of nature. While famine oppresses these miserable wretches, you hem and haw, feigning ignorance of their plight, and thus prolonging the agony. They come offering their very heart in exchange for food. And yet not only is your hand not stricken with paralysis for taking profits from such misfortune, but you haggle for even more! You wrangle so as to take much and give little in return, increasing the tragedy on every side for these wretches. Tears do not move you, groans do not soften your heart, but you remain adamant and unbending.

In everything you see gold, you imagine everything as gold; it is your dream when you sleep and your first thought when you awaken. Just as those who are out of their mind do not see reality, but rather imagine things out of their malady, thus also your soul, being seized with avarice, sees everything as gold or silver. You would rather see gold than the sun itself. You wish that everything could be transformed by nature and become gold, and for your part you intend to turn as many things into gold as you can.

5   To what lengths will you not go for gold? Your grain becomes gold for you, your wine solidifies into gold, your wool is transformed into gold; every exchange, every thought produces gold for you. Gold itself brings forth even more gold, multiplying itself through loans at interest. There is no satisfying the craving; no limit to the desire is to be found. We often permit immoderate children to gorge themselves on the things they desire the most, so that by means of overindulgence they might learn moderation. But greedy people are not like this; rather, the more they stuff themselves, the more they desire. "If riches flow in, do not set your heart on them."[12] But you check the flow and stop up the outlets. When riches are closed up like this so that they become stagnant, what do they do for you? Once wealth has been forcibly contained until it becomes a flood, it washes away all its embankments; it destroys the storehouses of the rich man and tears down his treasuries, charging like some kind of enemy warrior.

But will he indeed build larger storehouses? It seems doubtful that he will leave anything but ruins to his successors. For his departure from life came much sooner than his greedy plan to rebuild the storehouses could be accomplished. Let him meet the end that accords with his evil intent; but you, if you are persuaded by me, will throw open all the gates of your treasury, supplying liberal outlets for your wealth. Like a mighty river that is divided into many streams in order to irrigate the fertile soil, so also are those who give their wealth to be divided up and distributed in the houses of the poverty-stricken. Wells become more productive if they are drained completely, while they silt up if they are left standing. Thus wealth left idle is of no use to anyone, but put to use and exchanged it becomes fruitful and beneficial for the public.

How great is the praise of the recipients of beneficence; do not discount it! How great is the reward from the righteous Judge; do not doubt Him! Let the example of the rich man who is under examination accompany you everywhere. By keeping what he already had, while at the same time endeavoring to gain even more, he committed tomorrow's sins today. No suppliant had yet approached, but he showed his cruelty in advance. He had not yet gathered his harvest, yet he was already found guilty of avarice. The earth was welcoming all to its richness: it germinated the crops deep in the furrows, produced large clusters of grapes on the vine, made the olive tree bend under a vast quantity of fruit, and offered every delicious variety of the fruit tree. But the rich man was unwelcom-

[12]Ps 61.10 LXX.

ing and unfruitful; he did not even possess as yet, and already he begrudged the needy.

And besides, how many perils there are before the ingathering of the harvest! For hail may flatten the crops, searing heat may snatch them out of hand, or unseasonable rain may ruin them as it pours down from the clouds. Yet you do not pray to the Lord to complete the good work. Rather, by anticipation you make yourself unworthy of receiving what has just begun to sprout.

6 Though you speak to yourself in secret, your words are examined in heaven. Thus, it is from heaven that you will receive your reply. But what sort of things do you say to yourself? "Soul, you have ample goods laid up for many years; relax, eat, drink, and be merry day after day." Oh, what senselessness! If you had the soul of a pig, what better news could you have given it? Are you really so animal-like, so devoid of understanding as to what is good for the soul, that you offer it the foods of the flesh and serve it things that go into the latrine? If your soul possesses virtue, if it is full of good works and dwells near to God, then indeed it has "many good things," and should rejoice with the soul's own pure joy. But because you consider only earthly things and have made your belly into a god, because you are entirely fleshly and enslaved by passions, hear the fitting appellation that is given to you, not by any human being, but by the Lord Himself: "You fool! This very night your life is being demanded of you. And the things you have prepared, whose will they be?" Worse even than eternal punishment is this scorn on account of your folly.

In just a little while, his life will be snatched away, and what is he thinking? "I will pull down my barns and build larger ones." Well done, I would say for my part. The treasuries of injustice well deserve to be torn down. With your own hands, raze these misbegotten structures. Destroy the granaries from which no one has ever gone away satisfied. Demolish every storehouse of greed, pull down the roofs, tear away the walls, expose the moldering grain to the sunlight, lead forth from prison the fettered wealth, vanquish the gloomy vaults of Mammon.

"I will pull down my barns and build larger ones." But if you fill these larger ones, what do you intend to do next? Will you tear them down yet again only to build them up once more? What could be more ridiculous than this incessant toil, laboring to build and then laboring to tear down again? If you want storehouses, you have them in the stomachs of the poor. Lay up for yourself treasure in heaven. The things deposited there are not devoured by moths, nor are they spoiled by corruption, nor do thieves break in and steal them. But you reply, "I will give to the needy when I have filled the second set of barns." You are so sure that the years of your life will be many; beware, lest death the pursuer catch up to you sooner than you expect! And even your promise is not a token of goodness, but rather a sign of your evil intent. For you promise, not so that you might give in the future, but rather so that you might evade responsibility in the present. At this very moment, what prevents you from giving? Are not the needy near at hand? Are not your barns already full? Is not your heavenly reward waiting? Is not the commandment crystal clear? The hungry are perishing, the naked are freezing to death, the debtors are unable to breathe, and will you put off showing mercy until tomorrow? Listen to Solomon: "Do not say to your neighbor, 'Go, and come again, tomorrow I will give it.'"[13] You do not know what tomorrow will bring.

How many precepts you ignore, since your ears are plugged with avarice! How much gratitude you ought to have shown to your Benefactor, how joyful and radiant you ought to have been that you are not one of those who crowd in at others' doors, but rather others are knocking at your door. But now you lower your eyes and quicken your step, muttering hasty responses, lest anyone pry some small coin from your grasp. You know how to say only one thing: "I do not have, I cannot give, I myself am poor." You are poor indeed and bereft of all goodness: poor in love, poor in kindness, poor in

[13]Prov 3.28.

faith towards God, poor in eternal hope. Make your brothers and
sisters sharers of your grain; give to the needy today what rots away
tomorrow. Truly, this is the worst kind of avarice: not even to share
perishable goods with those in need.

7   "But whom do I treat unjustly," you say, "by keeping what is my
own?" Tell me, what is your own? What did you bring into this life?
From where did you receive it? It is as if someone were to take the
first seat in the theater, then bar everyone else from attending, so
that one person alone enjoys what is offered for the benefit of all in
common—this is what the rich do. They seize common goods before
others have the opportunity, then claim them as their own by right of
preemption. For if we all took only what was necessary to satisfy our
own needs, giving the rest to those who lack, no one would be rich,
no one would be poor, and no one would be in need.

Did you not come forth naked from the womb, and will you not
return naked to the earth? Where then did you obtain your belongings? If you say that you acquired them by chance, then you deny
God, since you neither recognize your Creator, nor are you grateful
to the One who gave these things to you. But if you acknowledge that
they were given to you by God, then tell me, for what purpose did
you receive them? Is God unjust, when He distributes to us unequally
the things that are necessary for life? Why then are you wealthy while
another is poor? Why else, but so that you might receive the reward
of benevolence and faithful stewardship, while the poor are honored
for patient endurance in their struggles? But you, stuffing everything
into the bottomless pockets of your greed, assume that you wrong
no one; yet how many do you in fact dispossess?

Who are the greedy? Those who are not satisfied with what suf-
fices for their own needs. Who are the robbers? Those who take for
themselves what rightfully belongs to everyone. And you, are you
not greedy? Are you not a robber? The things you received in trust
as a stewardship, have you not appropriated them for yourself? Is not
the person who strips another of clothing called a thief? And those

who do not clothe the naked when they have the power to do so, should they not be called the same? The bread you are holding back is for the hungry, the clothes you keep put away are for the naked, the shoes that are rotting away with disuse are for those who have none, the silver you keep buried in the earth is for the needy. You are thus guilty of injustice toward as many as you might have aided, and did not.

8 "These are fine words," you say, "but gold is finer still." It is just as in the case of those who converse with the licentious concerning chastity: while they are condemning immorality, those whom they address are burning with desire at the reminder. How can I bring the sufferings of the poor to your attention, so that you might realize from what misery you are collecting riches for yourself? Oh, how desirable will these words appear to you on the day of judgment: "Come, you that are blessed by my Father, inherit the kingdom prepared for you from the foundation of the world; for I was hungry and you gave me food, I was thirsty and you gave me something to drink, I was naked and you gave me clothing."[14] But how great will be the trembling, the sweat, and the darkness that surround you when you hear the sentence: "You that are accursed, depart from me into the eternal fire prepared for the devil and his angels; for I was hungry and you gave me no food, I was thirsty and you gave me nothing to drink, I was naked and you did not give me clothing."[15] Moreover, those who are under accusation in this passage are not those who have stolen anything; these charges are rather leveled against those who have not shared with others.

I have spoken words that I thought would be profitable for you. For you who are persuaded, the promised good things that await are evident; for you who disobey, the threatened punishments have been plainly written down. I hope that you may escape these chastisements by making a better choice than the rich man, so that your

[14] Mt 25.34–36.
[15] Mt 25.41–43.

own riches may become a ransom for you, and you may progress toward the good things that have been prepared for us in heaven, by the grace of the One who calls us all into His Kingdom, to whom be glory and dominion forever and ever. Amen.

from threat of
punishment to blame,
judgment

In Time of Famine and Drought

The lion has roared; who will not fear? The Lord God has spoken; who can but prophesy?

Amos 3.8

1   Let us begin our oration with this prophecy, and as we endeavor to offer sound advice and counsel for the benefit of all, let us take as our helper the God-bearing prophet Amos, who healed afflictions like those we now suffer. In former times, when the people abandoned the piety of their forebears and disregarded the careful observance of the Law, slipping gradually into the service of the idols, this same prophet became a preacher of repentance, urging the people to turn back and warning them of the coming punishment. I pray that I too might receive some measure of his prophetic zeal as described in the ancient narrative, though I have no desire to see the outcome of events that followed in those days. The people were rebellious; they were like a stiff-necked and stubborn colt that has caught the bit in its teeth and so cannot be properly guided, but rather turns aside from the right path, prancing wildly, rearing and snorting as it struggles against the one who holds the reins, so that in the end it falls off a cliff into a ravine, suffering deserved ruin for its disobedience.

May this not be the result in our case, my children, whose father I have become through the gospel,[1] and whom I have swathed with the blessing of my own hands. Rather, let us be thoughtful listeners with souls ready to obey, willing to accept exhortation, submitting

[1]Cf. 1 Cor 4.15.

73

to the one who speaks like wax beneath the seal. Thus, from a single entreaty I will reap a harvest of rejoicing for my efforts, and on the day when we are delivered from this calamity, you will offer praises for my exhortation. The souls of the listeners are now poised in anticipation, ready to hear, while the expected pronouncement is delayed; what, then, is the subject of today's discourse?

2   Brothers and sisters, we see how the heavens have grown hard and unyielding, naked and bereft of clouds, while the clear blue sky makes an unwelcome and distressing appearance. In the past, we used to long for even a glimpse of the sky when it remained covered with clouds for long intervals, leaving us in darkness and shadow. The earth is completely dried up, terrible to see, barren and utterly unsuitable for planting. Its surface is cracked and broken up by the unrelenting glare of the sun. Abundant and reliable springs have failed us, and the flow of the great rivers has dried up; tiny children now play within their banks, while women carrying burdens cross them easily. Many have nothing to drink and are in danger of perishing from thirst. They are like new Israelites, seeking a new Moses with a wonder-working staff, so that the striking of stones may once again cure the thirst of the people, and miraculous clouds may again drop unaccustomed food, the manna, for human beings. Let us take care, then, that we do not become for subsequent generations a byword of starvation and punishment.

I saw the fields and wept bitterly for their unfruitfulness; I poured out my lament, since the rain does not pour down upon us. Some of the seeds dried up without germinating, buried by the plow beneath clumps of dried earth. The rest, after just beginning to take root and sprout, were withered by the hot wind in a manner pitiful to see. Thus, someone might now aptly invert the words of the Gospel and say, "the laborers are many, but the harvest is scant." Farmers sit in their fields and clasp their hands against their knees—this, of course, is the posture of those who mourn—weeping for their wasted efforts. They look at their young children and burst into tears, they see their wives and wail with grief, as they stroke and caress the dried-up crops, racked with sobs like parents who lose their children in the flower of youth.

Let us listen again to the same prophet whom we heard at the beginning of our discourse. "And I also withheld the rain from you when there were still three months to the harvest; I would send rain on one city, and send no rain on another city; one field would be rained upon, and the field on which it did not rain withered; so two or three towns wandered to one town to drink water, and were not satisfied, because you did not return to me, says the Lord."[2] We should learn, then, that it is because we have turned away from the Lord and disregarded His ways that God has inflicted these wounds upon us. He does not seek to destroy us, but rather endeavors to turn us back to the right way, just as good parents who care for their children are stern and rebuke them when they do wrong, not because they wish them harm, but rather desiring to lead them from childish negligence and the sins of youth to mature attentiveness.

See, now, how the multitude of our sins has altered the course of the year and changed the character of the seasons, producing these unusual temperatures. The winter did not produce alternating wetness and dryness as usual, but rather kept all its moisture frozen into ice, and so passed with no sign of snow or rain. The spring, moreover, showed only one side of its nature, namely warmth, but without any corresponding share of wetness. Scorching heat and biting frost, exceeding their boundaries in an unprecedented way, conspired to wreak severe damage upon human beings, even depriving them of life itself. What then is the cause of this disorder, this confusion? What brought about this change in the nature of the seasons? Let us investigate this question as those who have intelligence; as rational beings let us reason. Has the one who governs all ceased to exist? Or has the master artisan forgotten his providential care? Has he been stripped of his power and authority? Or, if he still possesses his might and retains his dominion, has he lapsed

[2] Am 4.7–8.

Dying God? Retreating? cruel?

into callousness and turned his great goodness and providence into misanthropy?

A wise person would not say this. Rather, the reason why our needs are not provided for as usual is plain and obvious: we do not share what we receive with others. We praise beneficence, while we deprive the needy of it. When we were slaves, we were set free, yet we feel no compassion for our fellow slaves. When we were hungry, we were fed, yet we neglect the needy. Though we have a God who is generous and lacks nothing, we have become grudging and unsociable towards the poor. Our sheep give birth to many lambs, yet there are more people who go about naked than there are shorn sheep. Our storehouses groan with plenty, yet we have no mercy on those who groan with want. For this reason we are threatened with righteous judgment. This is why God does not open his hand: because we have closed up our hearts towards our brothers and sisters. This is why the fields are arid: because love has dried up.

what was the poor like in Basil's time

Lack of Charity as explanation → punishment

3 The voices of those who pray disperse vainly in the air, since we do not listen to those who entreat our help. Is this what you call prayer and supplication? The men, except for a few, occupy themselves with commerce, while the women assist them in the service of Mammon. Few there are who have gathered to pray with me, and those who have come are drowsy, yawning, peering around incessantly, counting the minutes until the cantor finishes the verses, until they are released from church and the duty of prayer as from a dungeon. The little children, who have put away their writing tablets in the schools and now add their voices to ours, approach the occasion as release and enjoyment. They turn our sorrow into a festival, since they are set free for a little while from the discipline of the teacher and the duty of their lessons. The masses of adults, on the other hand, the people entangled in sins, hurry about the city free and easy and cheerful, even though they are responsible for these ills; they are the ones who have wrought and set in motion this catastrophe. Blameless and innocent babes make haste to assemble for confession, yet neither are they to blame for the present distress, nor do they possess the understanding or the capacity for extended prayer. You who are defiled with sins, come and join me in the assembly; prostrate yourselves and groan and weep. Leave infants to pursuits appropriate to their age. When you stand accused, do you hide yourself and put forward the innocent in your place? Is the Judge so easily deceived, that you can substitute one face for another in this manner?

At any rate, you should be here present with your infant children; they should not be here by themselves. You see how the Ninevites entreated God with repentance as they mourned over their sins, which Jonah declared to them after surviving the sea and the whale. They did not put forward infants for repentance, while the adults took their ease and feasted sumptuously. Rather, the fast brought the sinful parents into subjection first of all, and the punishment afflicted the parents, while the infants by extension necessarily lamented also. Thus, a somber mood prevailed throughout all age groups, both those with understanding and those without—the former by choice, the latter by necessity. And God, seeing how they humbled themselves by condemning themselves to an exceedingly severe period of shared distress, had mercy upon their suffering and relieved their punishment, giving cause for rejoicing to those who so prudently repented.

Oh, what concerted repentance! What wise and intense affliction! They did not even leave the animals outside this discipline, but devised ways to compel them to cry out as well. They separated the calf from its mother and prevented the lamb from nursing; they took suckling children from the arms of their mothers. The mothers were placed in one enclosure, the children in another, calling out and replying to one another with plaintive voices. The hungry children sought the source of their milk, while the mothers were pierced by the sufferings of maternal instinct, and cried out to their children with anguished voices. Hungry infants screamed and gasped with the most urgent cries, while their mothers' hearts were tormented with the pangs of natural affection. And for this reason, the inspired word preserved the account of their repentance as a universal example of how to live.

The elders mourned on account of the threatened chastisement, tearing at their gray hairs. The young and those in their prime lamented even more fervently. Paupers groaned, while the rich forgot their comforts and put on sackcloth as befits those who mourn. The king of Nineveh himself turned his glory and splendor into shame. He put aside his crown and poured dust on his head; he cast off his royal garment and put on sackcloth. He left his high and exalted throne and crawled pitifully upon the ground. He forsook the luxuries that belonged to him as king in order to grieve together with the people; he became one of them, when he saw the wrath of the common Master of all.

4   This, then, is the appropriate mindset for wise servants. Such is the repentance of those who are entangled in sins. We, on the other hand, commit sins fervently, but repent in a slack and half-hearted manner. Who prays with streams of tears, so as to receive rainstorms and showers in due season? Who washes away sins in imitation of the blessed David, who rained tears upon his bed? Who washes the feet of strangers, rinsing away the dust of travel, so that in time of need that person might entreat God, seeking an end to the drought? Who supports the child without parents, so that God might in turn support the wheat, which is like an orphan battered down by the unseasonable winds? Who ministers to the widow afflicted by the hardships of life, so that the provisions we need might now be measured back to us? Tear up the unjust contract, so that sin might also be loosed. Wipe away the debt that bears high rates of interest, so that the earth may bear its usual fruits. For when gold and bronze and things that do not naturally reproduce give birth in a manner contrary to nature, then the earth which bears according to nature becomes barren and is sentenced to fruitlessness as a punishment to those who dwell there.

Let those who account greed a virtue and amass far more wealth than they actually need demonstrate now the value of the things they have treasured up. What good are they, if God is angry and prolongs His chastisement? Without the bread that was readily available in abundance until just yesterday, such people will soon turn an even paler shade of yellow than the gold they amass. Suppose there were no merchants, nor any grain in the storehouses: tell me, what then would be the value of even the heaviest purse? Will your purse not be buried together with you? Is not gold earth? Will it not be interred like worthless clay together with the clay of the body?

You have acquired all that you need except for one thing: the ability to feed yourself. With all your wealth, create even a single cloud! Contrive a means to produce a few raindrops; compel the earth to bear; loose with proud and arrogant wealth this catastrophe! Perhaps you should ask some pious person to pray for you, so that you may be granted relief from these tragic events—someone like Elijah the Tishbite: poor, gaunt, without shoes, without hearth or home, without means, covered by only a single garment, as Elijah was by his mantle, having prayer as a companion and self-control as a friend. And if by your entreaties you succeed in procuring the assistance of such a person, will you not utterly despise the possessions that burden you? Will you not spit upon gold? Will you not scatter silver, which you once called all-powerful and most beloved, like manure for the soil, recognizing it to be an ineffectual help in times of need?

It is on your account that this catastrophe was decreed, because you have but do not give, because you neglect the hungry, because you pay no heed to the plight of the miserable, because you show no mercy to those who prostrate themselves before you. Evil things come upon the people for the sake of a few; for one person's depravity the people are punished. Achar stole sacred things, and the whole company was scourged; Zimri committed fornication with Midianite women, and all Israel fell under judgment.

5   Let us now examine our lives, both individually and corporately; let us regard the drought as a guide leading us to remembrance of our sins. Let us sensibly utter the cry of the noble Job: "The hand of the Lord has touched me!"[3] Let us truly account this catastrophe as having occurred primarily because of our own sins. And if it is necessary to add yet another consideration, we should remember that sometimes such unfortunate events occur in people's lives as a test of soul. Those who are examined in this way, whether rich or poor, are thoroughly tried by difficult circumstances, for both rich and poor are tested through suffering. A time like this clearly demonstrates whether a person is indeed sociable and kindhearted, truly grateful, and not on the contrary a blasphemer, someone whose attitude shifts with the vicissitudes of life. I know many people—and I did not learn this from hearing, but rather know people by experience—who give thanks for the gifts of the Benefactor so long as their life proceeds with ease and prosperity, advancing, as it is said, moderately well if not perfectly. But let things turn to the opposite extreme—let the rich become poor, let the strength of the body be turned to weakness, let glory and splendor be reduced to shame and disgrace—and they become ungrateful. They pour out blasphemies, abandon prayer, and bitterly inveigh against God as against a debtor in arrears, instead of composing themselves like servants addressing a displeased master.

But enough of such thoughts. When you see that God does not provide as usual, you should think in this way: does not God have the power to grant us food? How could it be otherwise? He is the Lord of heaven and earth, the wise Steward of times and seasons. God set the boundaries of the seasons as they wax and wane, giving way to one another like a kind of well-ordered dance, so that the diversity of our needs might be satisfied by their endless variety. Thus, we see that the rainfall accrues during its proper season, while afterwards the earth receives warmth and coldness in appropriate mixtures throughout the course of the year. We even need a certain

[3]Job 19.21 LXX.

period of dryness. We know, then, that God is powerful. Since His might is thus evident and undisputed, is He perhaps deficient in goodness? But neither can this notion stand. If God were not good, what necessity could have persuaded Him to create human beings in the first place? Who could have compelled the Creator unwillingly to take dust and fashion such beauty from the dirt? Who could have prevailed upon Him to grant reason to human beings, as it were, out of necessity, so that thus impelled they might receive instruction in the arts, and learn to philosophize about the celestial realms, which cannot be apprehended through the senses?

If you think in this way, you will discover that God's goodness is still present and has not abandoned us even now. Otherwise, tell me, what would prevent there befalling us not a mere drought, but utter conflagration? What would prevent the sun from altering its usual course, drawing near to the terrestrial bodies and consuming in a moment all that we see? What would prevent fire from raining down from heaven, like that which punished the sinners of old?[4] Come to your senses, people! Do not behave like foolish children, who smash their teacher's writing tablets when they are rebuked, or rip apart their father's garments when he sends them away from the table to teach them a lesson, or scratch their own mother's face with their fingernails. Storms at sea test the mettle of the ship's captain, just as the arena does the athlete, the battle line the soldier, calamity the magnanimous, and times of trial the Christian. Sorrows try the soul as fire does gold.

Are you poor? Do not be discouraged. Too much sorrow becomes a source of sin: sadness inundates the mind, helplessness produces bewilderment, and perplexity generates ungrateful thoughts. Place your hope in God. Can it be that He does not understand your difficult position? If God has the ability to provide food, but delays in giving it, it is in order to test your resolution and examine your disposition, to see whether your inner state is like that of the licentious and senseless. So long as such people have food in

---

[4]I.e., Sodom and Gomorrah. Cf. Gen 19.1–29.

hunger as test of faith

their mouths, they gush with praise, flattery, and admiration. But if the setting of the table is only a little delayed, they begin hurling insults like stones at those whom they previously extolled as godlike on account of their satiety.

Open the Old or the New Testament, and you will discover in them many people who were fed in diverse ways. Elijah was on Mount Carmel, a high and uninhabited mountain, a solitary in solitude. For this righteous man, the soul was everything; his hope in God was his provision for life. The famine did not take his life, but rather the most greedy and gluttonous of the birds, the ravens, that customarily steal food from others, brought bread and served food to this righteous man. They altered their natural habits by the command of the Master, and thus became trustworthy guardians of the bread and meat. We learn from the sacred history how the ravens brought these provisions to this man. Daniel, the Israelite youth, was in the Babylonian pit, a captive during the deportation, yet free in his soul and mind. And what happened to him? The lions fasted in a manner contrary to their nature, and the prophet Habakkuk was transported through the air to bring him food, an angel conveying him together with the morsels. In order that this righteous man might not be hard pressed by hunger, Habakkuk was translated in but a moment of time over an area of land and sea stretching from Judea to Babylon.[5]

6 Moreover, consider what occurred in the case of the people in the wilderness, those whom Moses led. How were the things they needed to survive supplied during the forty years of wandering? There was no one to sow seed, nor any oxen to draw the plow, nor threshing floor, nor winepress, nor storehouse, yet they had food without planting or cultivation, and a stone provided streams of water where there had previously been none, gushing forth in time of need. I will not even try to enumerate one by one the instances of

[5]The story of Habakkuk bringing food to Daniel is found in Bel and the Dragon 1.32–39.

God's providence, the fatherly care he so often demonstrates towards humanity. You, then, persevere a little longer in the face of calamity, like the noble Job. Do not be turned aside by the billowing waves, nor cast off the precious cargo of virtue that you bear. Preserve gratitude like a precious deposit within your soul, and from it you will receive a double portion of delight. Remember the apostolic word, "Give thanks in all circumstances."[6]

Are you poor? You know someone who is even poorer. You have provisions for only ten days, but someone else has only enough for one day. As a good and generous person, redistribute your surplus to the needy.[7] Do not shrink from giving the little that you have; do not prefer your own benefit to remedying the common distress. And if you have only one remaining loaf of bread, and someone comes knocking at your door, bring forth the one loaf from your store, hold it heavenward, and say this prayer, which is not only generous on your part, but also calls forth the Lord's pity: "Lord, you see this one loaf, and you know the threat of starvation is imminent, but I place your commandment before my own well-being, and from the little I have I give to this famished brother. Give, then, in return to me your servant, since I am also in danger of starvation. I know your goodness, and am emboldened by your power. You do not delay your grace indefinitely, but distribute your gifts when you will." And when you have thus spoken and acted, the bread you have given from your straitened circumstances will become seed for sowing that bears a rich harvest, a promise of food, an envoy of mercy.

Say the word that was spoken by the widow of Zarephath when she was in similar circumstances; indeed, this is a good time to recall her story. "As the Lord lives, I have only enough in my house to feed myself and my children."[8] If you also give from your lack, you will have the vessel of oil ever flowing by the gift of mercy, and the

[6] 1 Thess 5.18.
[7] The Greek word here translated "redistribute" is ἐπανίσωσον, which literally means to "restore the balance," to take something from one side of the scale and move it to the other, a beautiful description of restorative or redistributive justice.
[8] Cf. 1 Kg 17.12ff.

inexhaustible jar of flour. For the faithful, the grace of God zealously imitates these vessels, ever poured out yet never exhausted, returning double for what is given. Lend, you who lack, to the rich God. Have faith in the one who always personally undertakes the cause of the oppressed, and makes recompense from his own resources. He is a trustworthy guarantor, since He has the treasures of land and sea at His disposal. And even if you were to ask for the return of the loan while you were sailing at sea, you would receive back the principal with interest in the very middle of the ocean. With God it is a matter of honor to give a generous return.

7   The disease of those who are starving, namely hunger, is a terrible form of suffering. Hunger is the most severe of human maladies, the very worst kind of death. The other hazards to human life do not involve extended torment: whether in the case of death by the sword, which brings about a swift end, or roaring flames, which swiftly extinguish life, or wild beasts, that tear one limb from limb with their teeth, the interval of suffering is relatively brief. But starvation prolongs the pain and draws out the agony, so that sickness is ensconced and lurks within the body, while death is ever present yet ever delayed. The body becomes dehydrated, its temperature drops, its bulk dwindles, its strength wastes away. Skin clings to bone like a spider's web. The flesh loses its natural coloration: its ruddiness fades as the flow of blood decreases, while the alabaster of the skin turns discolored and dark. The body takes on a mottled hue, with yellow and black patches mingling in a manner terrible to see. The knees can no longer support the weight of the body, but are forced to drag along behind. The voice grows weak and feeble. The eyes become diseased and are rendered useless, sunken in their sockets like fruits that shrivel up in their skins. The belly is empty, shrunken to nothing, possessing neither girth nor the natural tone of the bowels, so that the bones of the spine are visible from the front.

How many torments does the one who neglects such a body deserve? What extreme of cruelty does such a person not surpass?

Does not someone like this deserve to be numbered among the savage beasts, being accounted accursed and murderous? For whoever has the ability to remedy the suffering of others, but chooses rather to withhold aid out of selfish motives, may properly be judged the equivalent of a murderer.

In certain circumstances, the torments of hunger have even compelled people to transgress the boundaries of nature, causing one human being to devour the body of another, even a mother that of her own child, so that in a horrible manner she receives back into her own body that which she bore. Such a tragic instance is recorded for us in the history of the Jews written by the learned Josephus,[9] who describes the severe suffering that seized the inhabitants of Jerusalem, a just sentence inflicted upon them for their impiety towards the Lord.

You see how God, our God Himself, frequently passes over other forms of suffering, but is filled with sympathy and compassion for the hungry. "I have compassion," says the Lord, "for the crowd."[10] Thus also at the Last Judgment, when the Lord shall call the righteous, the one who shares will occupy the first rank. The one who feeds others will be foremost among those honored; the one who gives bread will be summoned first of all; the person who is good and gives generously will enter into eternal life before the rest. But the unsociable and stingy will be the first to be given over to the eternal fire.

The times are calling you to return to the mother of the commandments. Take exceeding care, lest the opportunity of celebration and reward pass you by. Time flows onward, and does not wait for the one who delays. The days hasten, passing by the one who hesitates. There is no stopping the flow of a river; one can only draw forth water for use as it approaches and before it passes by. In the same way, it is not possible to halt time, which hurtles onward in its appointed intervals, nor to turn it back once it is past; one can only

[9]Josephus *Jewish War* 6.3.4.
[10]Mt 15.32.

seize it as it approaches. For this reason, take hold of the commandment and discharge it before the opportunity flees away; wrap your
arms around it and hold it tightly from all sides. Give but a little,
and you will gain much; undo the primal sin by sharing your food.
Just as Adam transmitted sin by eating wrongfully, so we wipe away
the treacherous food when we remedy the need and hunger of our
brothers and sisters.

8   Listen, O people! Hear me, O Christians! These things the
Lord says, not addressing the people with His own voice, but rather
proclaiming the message through the mouths of His servants as
through musical instruments. Let not we who are reasonable show
ourselves to be more savage than the unreasoning animals. For even
the animals use in common the plants that grow naturally from the
earth. Flocks of sheep graze together upon the same hillside, herds of
horses feed upon the same plain, and all living creatures permit each
other to satisfy their need for food. But we hoard what is common,
and keep for ourselves what belongs to many others.

We should be put to shame by what has been recorded concerning the pagan Greeks. For some of them, a law of philanthropy
dictated a single table and common meals, so that many different
people might almost be regarded as one household. But let us dispense with those outside the Church, and proceed to the example
of the three thousand mentioned in the Book of Acts.[11] Let us zealously imitate the early Christian community, where everything was
held in common—life, soul, concord, a common table, indivisible
kinship—while unfeigned love constituted many bodies as one and
joined many souls into a single harmonious whole. You can find
numerous examples of such love for others in both the Old Testament and the New. If you see an elderly person hungry, invite him
to come and eat, as Joseph did Jacob. If you discover your enemy
hard pressed, do not add desire for vengeance to the wrath which
already possesses you, but rather feed him as Joseph fed the brothers

[11]Cf. Acts 2.41 ff.

who sold him. If you encounter a haggard youth, you should weep as Joseph did for Benjamin, the son of Jacob's old age. It may be that you are troubled by greed, as Joseph was troubled by the wife of Potiphar. Greed tugs at your garments, urging you to disregard the commandment and to love gold and fine apparel rather than the injunction of the Master. When a thought appears that opposes the commandment and entices the prudent mind towards the love of money, a thought that compels you to neglect the love of others and clings to you tenaciously, then you also should cast aside your clothing and depart incensed. Remain faithful to the Lord, as Joseph did to his master Potiphar. Endure want for one year, as Joseph did for seven.

Do not give everything over to self-indulgence; save something for the soul as well. Consider yourself to have two daughters: the enjoyment of this life, and the life to come in the heavens. If you do not want to give everything to the better cause, at least divide your possessions equally between the immoderate child and the prudent one. Do not enrich the present life while leaving the other naked and clothed in rags. Rather, when the time comes for you to stand before Christ and appear in the presence of the Judge, let the life of virtue have her bridal raiment and invitation ready. Do not present the bride unkempt and shabbily attired, lest when he beholds her the Bridegroom should turn his face away with loathing at the sight and cancel the engagement. Rather, preserve the splendor of the appointed day by sending her dressed in appropriate adornment, so that she may light her lamp together with the prudent virgins, having the inextinguishable light of knowledge, and not lacking the oil of righteous deeds. Then the God-inspired prophecy will be confirmed through actions, and the word that was spoken will aptly befit your own soul: "The queen stood at your right hand clothed in a garment woven of gold and beautifully arrayed. Hear, O daughter, consider and incline your ear; forget your people and your father's house, and the King will desire your beauty."[12] These things the Psalmist

[12] Ps 44.9–11 LXX.

prophesied generally, foreseeing the beauty of the entire body, but they also apply specifically to each particular soul, since the Church is a whole comprised of individual members.

9   Consider carefully, I ask you, both the present and the future; do not betray the latter from a shameful motive of profit. The body, your outward manifestation in this life, will forsake you in the end. At the appearance of the expected Judge—and come He most certainly will—you will shut yourself out of the distribution of heavenly glory and honor. Instead of the enduring and blessed life, you will enter into the unquenchable fire of hell and bitter ages of agony. Do not think that I am conjuring up imaginary stories of terrible creatures in order to frighten you, like a mother or some kind of nursemaid, who are accustomed to silencing little children who wail incessantly and inconsolably with such fanciful tales. These things are not myth, but reality foretold by the voice of truth. Know assuredly, then, in accordance with the Gospel proclamation, "not one letter, not one stroke of a letter, will pass from the law until all is accomplished."[13] The body that has disintegrated in the grave will arise, and will be reunited with the very same soul from which it was separated by death. Then a careful examination of each person's life will take place, in which no others will testify, but rather one's own conscience will bear witness. Everyone will then receive due reward from the just Judge. To Him is due glory, dominion, and worship forever and ever. Amen.

[13]Mt 5.18.

Against Those Who Lend at Interest

They do not lend money at interest . . .

Psalm 14.5 LXX

1   Yesterday, as we were explaining Psalm 14, time did not permit us to reach the end of our discourse. Today, however, we come like good-natured debtors, ready to repay the remainder owing from yesterday's discussion. The rest of the Psalm is so short, however, that upon hearing it, one might think nothing of importance had been omitted; most of you have probably not even noticed that anything was left out. And yet recognizing that this brief verse concerns matters of great interest to us, it seemed best not to lose the profit of examining it. When the prophet wished to describe in words those who have attained perfection, those who are about to attain to everlasting life, he reckoned among their noble works the following: "They do not lend money at interest." This sin is denounced in many places in Scripture. Ezekiel accounts the taking of interest and receiving back more than one gave as being among the greatest evils,[1] and the Law specifically forbids this practice: "You shall not charge interest to your relative or your neighbor."[2] And again the Scripture says, "Guile upon guile, and interest upon interest,"[3] and a certain Psalm moreover says regarding a city that prospers amidst a multitude of evils, "Interest-taking and guile are never absent from its squares."[4] And now, the prophet identifies this very thing as the

[1] Cf. Ezek 22.12, "You take both advance interest and accrued interest, and make gain of your neighbors by extortion."
[2] Deut 23.20 LXX.
[3] Jer 9.6 LXX.
[4] Ps. 54.12 LXX.

characteristic of human perfection, saying, "They do not lend money at interest."

For in truth it is the height of inhumanity that those who do not have enough even for basic necessities should be compelled to seek a loan in order to survive, while others, not being satisfied with the return of the principal, should turn the misfortune of the poor to their own advantage and reap a bountiful harvest. Thus, the Lord explicitly commanded us, saying, "Do not refuse anyone who wants to borrow from you."[5] But the lover of money, when he sees someone prostrate at his feet, pleading—a person in this predicament will say anything, will stoop to any abasement—shows no mercy to the one who acts in such an undignified manner. He does not consider human nature, gives in to no entreaty, but stands cruel and unwavering, not yielding to pleas, not moved by tears, steadfast in his denial. He swears up and down, even calling down curses upon himself, that he is at a complete loss for funds, and that he too is searching for someone from whom to procure a loan. He confirms the falsehood with an oath, thus acquiring perjury as an evil fringe benefit of misanthropy. When, however, the one seeking the loan mentions rates of interest and names collateral, then he winks and smiles, suddenly recalling some old family acquaintance, and calls him "friend" and "neighbor." He says, "Let me see if I can find some money set aside somewhere. I have here a deposit entrusted to me by a friend for trading, but he set heavy terms of interest on it. For you, however, I will reduce the rate somewhat and lend it to you at lower interest." And with this subterfuge, cozying up to the wretch and baiting the hook with his words, he binds him fast with contracts and departs, depriving him of freedom even more than the poverty that already oppressed him. The one who has made himself liable for rates of interest he cannot pay has incurred self-inflicted slavery for life.

Tell me, do you really seek riches and financial gain from the destitute? If this person had the resources to make you even wealthier, why did he come begging to your door? He came seeking an ally,

[5]Mt 5.42.

but found an enemy. He came seeking medicine, and stumbled onto poison. Though you have an obligation to remedy the poverty of someone like this, instead you increase the need, seeking a harvest from the desert. It is as if a doctor were to go to the diseased, and instead of restoring them to health, were rather to rob them of the last remnant of their strength. Thus, you make the hardships of the miserable an occasion for profit. And just as farmers hope for rain so as to multiply their crops, so you eagerly seek out deprivation and want, so that your money might produce a better return. Do you not know that you are taking in an even greater yield of sins than the increase of wealth you hope to receive through interest? The one who seeks the loan is caught in a predicament. When he looks to his poverty, he despairs of ever making repayment, but when he looks to his present condition of need, he makes bold to seek the loan. In the end, the borrower is defeated, bowed into submission by want, while the lender departs victorious, having secured his position with contracts and pledges.

2   After receiving the money, on the first day he is joyful and festive, decked out in borrowed splendor, the change in his circumstances in clear evidence. There is a richly laden table and lavish clothing. Even the servants have brightened in their appearance. He is surrounded by multitudes of flatterers and drinking companions, hovering around the house like swarms of drones. But as the money begins to dwindle, the interest ever increasing as time passes, the nights do not bring rest to him, nor does the coming of the day bring joy, nor does the sunrise seem beautiful. Rather, he despises his own life and loathes the days as they hasten onwards towards the appointed day of repayment, and hates the months as producers of interest. If he lies down, in his sleep he sees the lender as a nightmare floating over his head. If he wakes up, the interest consumes his thoughts and is a constant source of worry. "When lender and debtor meet one another, the Lord visits them both."[6] The one rushes like a hound to

[6]Prov 29.13 LXX.

the hunt, while the other quails like quarry at the pursuit. Poverty robs him of his courage. Both have the sums at their fingertips, since the one rejoices at the increasing interest, while the other groans at the additional misfortune.

"Drink water at your own cistern";[7] that is, look to your own means. Do not turn to other springs, but draw forth from your own springs the comforts of life. Do you have utensils of bronze, clothing, a beast of burden, vessels for all your needs? Sell them all; choose to give up everything rather than your freedom. "But," says the borrower, "I am ashamed to put them up for public sale." What will you do, when in just a little while someone else brings your possessions forward and auctions them off, disposing of them at bargain prices before your very eyes? Do not turn to other doorways. Truly, "the stranger's well is narrow."[8] It is better to take care of your needs little by little with your own devices, than to be raised up all at once by outside means, only to be completely stripped of everything you have. If, then, you have anything at all to sell, why do you not alleviate your need with these resources? And if, on the other hand, you have nothing with which to make repayment, then you are remedying evil with more evil. Do not allow the moneylender to lay siege to you. Do not allow yourself to be tracked and hunted down like some kind of prey.

Borrowing is the origin of falsehood, the source of ingratitude, unkindness, perjury. A person says one thing when seeking to borrow and another when the loan is demanded back. "Would that I had never met you! By now I would have found some other means of relieving my need. Did you not thrust the money into my hands against my will? Your gold was alloyed with copper, and your coins were counterfeit." If the lender is your friend, do not ruin the friendship. If the lender is an enemy, do not allow yourself to fall into the hands of your foe. For a short time you will rejoice in what does not belong to you, but afterwards you will lose the family inheritance.

[7]Prov 5.15.
[8]Prov 23.27 LXX.

Now you are poor, but free. By borrowing, however, you will not become rich, and you will surrender your freedom. The borrower is a slave to the lender, a slave rendering involuntary service for the profit of another. Dogs become tame if you feed them, but when the creditor receives back what was borrowed, he becomes even more enraged. He does not stop his howling, but on the contrary, demands even more. Although you swear you will pay, he does not believe you. He pries into your private affairs, and inquires about your transactions. If you emerge from your home, he seizes you and drags you away; if you hide yourself within, he stands outside and pounds at the door. He shames you before your spouse, treats you disgracefully in front of your friends, seizes you by the throat in public places. Even a chance meeting at a festival is a disaster; he makes life unbearable.

"But the need is great," says the borrower, "and there are no other financial resources available." Your poverty will catch up to you like a speedy runner,[9] and the same lack will be with you again, and more. The loan is not complete deliverance; it merely provides a short respite from your helpless situation. Let us suffer today the difficulties of want, and not defer them until tomorrow. If you do not borrow, then your poverty will be the same tomorrow as it was today. But if you borrow, you make your troubles even worse, exacerbating poverty with rates of interest. Now, no one blames you for being poor, since this misfortune came upon you involuntarily. But if you make yourself liable for loans at interest, then everyone will fault you for your lack of good judgment.

3   Let us therefore not drag along behind us, together with the evils that befall us involuntarily, the burden of an evil freely chosen through our own foolishness. It is the sign of an infantile mind not to care for oneself with the resources that are available, but rather to partake of something clearly and undeniably harmful while trusting in unseen hopes. Consider, now, how you will repay the debt. From the sum you received? But it is not sufficient for both your needs and

[9]Cf. Prov 24.34 LXX.

repayment. And if you take into account the rate of interest, how will the funds be multiplied to such an extent that one portion takes care of your needs, while another serves to repay the principal, not to mention the interest that is accruing? So we agree that you will not repay the loan from the amount you received. How else, then? Let us wait for these hoped-for solutions to materialize, and not come like fish to the bait. For just as a fish swallows the hook together with the bait, so also we are pierced with interest rates for the sake of money. There is no shame in poverty. Why then do we bring the disgrace of indebtedness onto ourselves? No one can heal wounds with more wounds, nor remedy evil with more evil, nor alleviate poverty with loans at interest. Are you rich? Do not borrow. Are you poor? Do not borrow. If you are well off, you have no need of the loan; if you have nothing, you will not be able to repay it. Do not give your life over to bitter regret, lest you count the days before you took the loan as the happiest of your life.

There is one thing in which we poor differ from the rich: freedom from care. We laugh them to scorn when they lie awake at night while we sleep, and when they are constantly tense and worrying we are relaxed and at ease. But the debtor is both poor and full of cares, awake by night, still awake when the day comes, fretting all the time. At one moment he calculates the value of his own property, at another that of the luxurious houses, the fields of the wealthy, the clothing of those he happens to meet, the furnishings of those who host entertainments. "If these things were mine," he says, "I would have sold so much, and paid off both the loan and the interest." Such ideas are fixed in his heart by night, and overwhelm his thoughts by day. If you knock at his door, the debtor is underneath the bed in a flash. His heart pounds if someone enters the room suddenly. If a dog barks, he breaks out in a sweat, seized with terror, and looks for someplace to hide. As the appointed day of repayment draws near, he weighs in his mind what deceit would be best, with what fabricated excuse to elude the lender. Do not only imagine yourself receiving the loan, but also paying it back.

To what manner of quickly reproducing beast are you yoking yourself? It is said that rabbits give birth and breed again while still nursing their young. And for those who set rates of interest, their money is loaned out and bears interest and produces even more. You did not even have the money in your hands, and already the lender was demanding the interest payment for the current month. And when this was loaned to you as well, it brought forth more evil, and still more, evil without end. It is from the tendency to multiply that this kind of greed derives its name.[10] For it seems to me that loans are said to "bear" interest on account of the great fecundity of evil. How else? Or perhaps interest is said to "bear" on account of the pains and travails which it naturally produces in the souls of those who borrow. The appointed day of repayment is ever present in the minds of those who are indebted, like labor pains to those who give birth. Interest upon interest—wicked children of wicked parents. The offspring of interest one might even call a "brood of vipers." It is said that vipers are born by eating their way through their mother's womb, and loans bear interest by devouring the houses of those who owe. Seeds take time to grow, and animals take time to fully mature, but interest is born today, and today begins to bear. Those animals that begin bearing at an early age also cease bearing early. But money immediately begins to multiply, and possesses limitless ability to reproduce. And every animal, once it reaches its proper size, stops growing. But the silver of the greedy never stops growing as time passes. And animals, once they have raised their young to maturity, cease bearing. But when it comes to borrowed silver, the newborn gives birth, and the elderly continues to bear. You should have nothing to do with this monstrous creature.

4   You behold the sun as a free person. Why do you begrudge the liberty you now enjoy? No boxer avoids the blows of an opponent as a borrower avoids chance encounters with the creditor, hiding his

---

[10]The Greek word τόκος (from the verb τίκτειν, "to bear") can mean either "offspring" or "interest."

face among the shadows of buildings and alleyways. "But how will I support myself?" such a person asks. You have hands, you have skills—hire yourself out as a laborer or a servant. Life has many possibilities and opportunities. Are you unable to work? Then beg from those who have means. Do you think it shameful to beg? You will be put to even greater shame if you default on a loan. In any case, I do not make these recommendations as if laying down a law, but rather to emphasize that anything is preferable to borrowing. The ant is able, without begging or borrowing, to feed itself, while the bee gives what remains of its own food to the queen,[11] which nature has given neither hands nor any skills. And you, a human being, the inventive animal, can you not find even one contrivance out of so many that are available for the preservation of life?

We may observe, moreover, that it is not those who are truly deprived who come to procure a loan, since the creditors have no confidence in their ability to repay; most borrowers are rather people who devote themselves to unconstrained expenditures and useless luxuries, those who serve the passionate desires of women. "I shall have fine clothing embroidered with gold," she says, "and it is only fitting that the children should have beautiful outfits as well. There shall be bright and colorful dress for all the slaves, and plenty of food for the table." The one who thus caters to the desires of a woman goes to the banker, and before using up the money received, exchanges one tyrant for another by constantly switching creditors, avoiding the accusation of poverty by extension of the evil. Just as those who suffer from edema give the impression of being overweight, so also such a person only appears to possess means, ever receiving and ever giving back, paying off the prior loan with the subsequent, and preserving good credit for future borrowing by extending the evil. Those who suffer from cholera constantly disgorge what they have eaten, and before their system is properly cleansed, they fill themselves up with a second portion, vomiting this up too with

---

[11]Lit. "the kings," perhaps a thinly veiled indictment of rulers who live off the efforts of others while making no contribution to the well-being of society.

terrible, racking pains—thus also are those who exchange interest for interest, taking out a second loan before discharging the first obligation. They are conceited for a time with things that do not belong to them, but afterwards mourn the loss of their own things. How many are destroyed by good things that are not their own? How many who became rich in a dream have gone down to utter ruin in reality? "But many," someone will say, "have become rich by taking out loans." Many more, I think, have ended by fastening a noose for themselves. You see those who have become rich, but you are not counting those who committed suicide, who could not bear to be publicly shamed before the creditors, who preferred death by hanging to a life of disgrace.

I have beheld a terrible spectacle: children of free birth being dragged to the auction block on account of the debts of their parents. Do you have no money to leave behind for your children? Do not take away their free birth as well! Preserve but one thing for them: the possession of their freedom, the same inheritance you received from your own parents. Children are not brought to court for the penury of their parents, but the debt of a parent leads straight to prison. Do not leave behind a ledger that will go down as a parental curse upon your children and grandchildren.

5   Listen, you rich, to the kind of counsel I am giving to the poor on account of your inhumanity: to remain in dreadful circumstances, rather than accepting the assistance offered by loans at interest. But if you took the Lord at his word, would there be any reason for such words? What is the counsel of the Master? "Lend to those from whom you do not hope to receive again."[12] "But what kind of loan is this," some will say, "that is not linked to a hope of return?" Only consider the meaning of these words, and you will wonder at the kindness of the Lawgiver. When you are about to give to a poor person on the Lord's account, that same gift is also a loan: it is a gift because you do not hope to receive it back again, but a loan because

[12]Lk 6.34.

the Master in his great beneficence undertakes to make repayment for the poor person. He receives a little in the guise of the poor, but gives back much on their behalf. "The one who has mercy on the poor lends to God."[13] Would you not like to have the Master of all as your guarantor for full repayment? If one of the rich people of the town were to make an agreement with you to pay off some others' loans, would you not take that person's pledge? And yet you do not allow God, the supreme repayer of debts, to do so. Give away that portion of your silver that is lying idle, do not burden it with interest rates, and it shall be well for you both: you will have the certainty that your money is well guarded, while the one who receives it will have the profit from its use. If you must seek a return on your investment, be satisfied with what comes from the Lord; he himself will pay the additional amount on behalf of the poor. You should expect the characteristics of philanthropy from the true Philanthropist. As it is, the interest you receive back shows every characteristic of extreme misanthropy. You profit from misery, you extract gain from tears, you oppress the naked, you beat down the starving. Mercy is nowhere to be found; there is no thought of kinship with those who suffer. And yet you call such gains the benefits of philanthropy! "Woe to those who call the bitter sweet and the sweet bitter,"[14] and to those who call misanthropy by the name of philanthropy. The riddles which Samson posed to his drinking companions were not like this: "Out of the eater came something to eat; out of the strong came something sweet,"[15] and out of the misanthropic person came philanthropy. "Grapes are not gathered from thorns, nor figs from thistles,"[16] nor philanthropy from interest rates. "Every bad tree bears bad fruit."[17]

Some lenders are called "hundred-percenters," some "ten-percenters"—these are dreadful names to hear. They are monthly

[13]Prov 19.17 LXX.
[14]Is 5.20 LXX.
[15]Judg 14.14.
[16]Mt 7.16.
[17]Mt 7.17.

demanders, like demons that cause seizures, afflicting the poor according to the cycles of the moon. Theirs is an evil act of giving, both for the giver and the receiver: the latter is ruined in terms of capital, the former in terms of the soul. The farmer who harvests the grain no longer searches for the seed that was sown and took root. But you have the harvest, and still do not give up on the original amount. You plant without soil; you harvest without seed. It is unknown, however, for whose benefit you are collecting it. The one who weeps in despair at the rate of interest is plainly before us, but the future of the one who is about to enjoy the wealth received from them is uncertain. It is unclear whether you will not rather leave this joy behind for others, while storing up an evil treasure of injustice for yourself. "Do not refuse anyone who wants to borrow from you,"[18] and "do not lend your money at interest";[19] these commandments from the Old and New Testaments were given so that you might learn what is for your benefit, and thus depart to the Lord with a good hope, receiving there the interest upon your good works, in Christ Jesus our Lord, to whom be glory and dominion forever and ever. Amen.

[18]Mt 5.42.
[19]Cf. Ps 14.5 LXX.

The Pseudo-Basilian Homily
On Mercy and Justice

The following text, attributed to Basil, has been included as an appendix to the present collection. It is most likely not by Basil himself, though it may have been delivered by one of his followers or a later monastic in the Basilian tradition. There are significant differences in style and content that distinguish this work from Basil's own. One particularly notable divergence is the way in which the author incorporates the story of the rich young man from the synoptic gospels and the commandment "sell your possessions and give to the poor." As was noted in the introduction, Basil rejects every attempt to develop a "two-tiered" approach to this commandment, insisting that all have the obligation to fulfill the law of love by sharing what they have with those who have less. Basil also insists that monastics should continue to fulfill this commandment by working at a trade in order to share their earnings with the poor. The author of the present work, on the other hand, uses this account to create precisely such a two-tiered structure, in which the "perfect followers" of Christ sell everything and give to the poor, while "the rest," who do not divest themselves of their possessions, content themselves with "allotment and sharing of what they have," even if this means giving only "some small thing." The former are freed from any further responsibility for rendering material assistance, since they have passed from "service to others by means of possessions" to the higher realm of "service by means of word and spirit." In an interesting twist of exegesis, the author interprets Jesus' words in Matthew 25.40,

"Inasmuch as you did it to one of the least of these my brothers and sisters, you did it to me" as assistance given to monastics by those who have not completely renounced their possessions. The commandment to aid the involuntary poor is thus superseded by the requirement to render assistance to the voluntary poor (i.e., monastics), who are "holy people" and "soldiers of Christ"; such patronage given by the wealthy to these perfect disciples is accounted as "reverence for Christ" and makes them "companions" and "co-workers" of Christ.

Despite these differences, however, appending this work to the Basilian corpus serves an important purpose, significantly expanding and augmenting certain aspects of Basil's thought. One of the fundamental premises of the work is that it is necessary to restore justice and equity to an unjust and imbalanced situation before one can even speak of showing mercy. In his sermons on social themes, Basil spends a great deal of time asking those who possess great means to consider how they might charitably redistribute their surpluses; he devotes less attention, however, to the question of how this wealth was obtained. Basil is prone to speak of "keeping" wealth while others have less than they need to live as injustice. The author of the present work, on the other hand, extends the principle of justice to include how this wealth is acquired. Those who obtain their wealth through injustice may not simply return part of what has been taken from the poor and call it "charity." This is especially true in relationships which involve an imbalance of power, where the temptation to exploitation and abuse is particularly great. Those who desire to assist the needy are instructed first to examine themselves "in order to make certain that they have not wielded power over the poor, or used force against the weak, or committed extortion against those in a subordinate position." The author thus suggests that the elimination of injustice demands not only the redistribution of material resources, but also an examination of how power is wielded within society.

In Basil's writings, one finds a great deal of emphasis on the requirement to show mercy to the needy neighbor. The present work enriches Basil's concept of "restoring the balance" by emphasizing that

mercy and justice must remain in a constant and fruitful tension: the
hearers are called to "possess with justice and dispense with mercy."

ON MERCY AND JUSTICE[1]

The world that forgets God, brothers and sisters, is ruled by injustice
toward neighbors and inhumanity toward the weak. As the apostle
Paul says, "Since they did not see fit to acknowledge God, God gave
them up to a debased mind and to things that should not be done.
They were filled with every kind of wickedness, evil, covetousness,
malice. Full of envy, murder, strife, deceit, craftiness, they are gos-
sips, slanderers, God-haters, insolent, haughty, boastful, inventors
of evil, rebellious toward parents, foolish, faithless, heartless, ruth-
less."[2] God restores such people to proper reverence, teaching them
to abstain from evil and pursue mercy toward their neighbors. Just
as the Prophet Isaiah, speaking on behalf of God, taught, "Cease to
do evil, learn to do good."[3] The Mosaic Law also contained many
commandments regarding not harming one's neighbor, as well as
many precepts enjoining kindness and mercy. If someone abandons
the practice of the one, the other will not suffice for that person's
restoration. Acts of charity made from unjust gains are not acceptable to God, nor are those who refrain from injustice praiseworthy
if they do not share what they have. It is written concerning those
who commit injustice and then attempt to offer gifts to God, "The
sacrifice of the wicked is an abomination to the Lord."[4] With regard
to those who fail to show mercy, however, it says, "If you close your
ear to the cry of the poor, you will cry out and not be heard."[5]

[1]In the Greek text, the homily begins with the injunction "Father, bless," suggesting a monastic context and the presence of an abbot.
[2]Rom 1.28–30.
[3]Is 1.16–17.
[4]Prov 15.8.
[5]Prov 21.13.

It is for this reason that Proverbs instructs, "Honor the Lord with your just labors, and offer as first fruits your righteous works."[6] But if you plan to make an offering to God out of the fruits of injustice and exploitation, you should know that it would be better for you neither to possess such things nor to make any offering from them. A pure gift gives wings to prayer; as it is written, "The prayers of the upright are acceptable to God."[7] Conversely, if you possess what you have as a result of just labor, yet make no offerings to God for the support of the poor, exploitation is reckoned against you, according to what was spoken by the prophet Malachi, "The first fruits and tithes remain in your possession, and the gains of exploitation shall be in your house."[8]

It is therefore necessary for you to blend mercy and justice, possessing with justice and dispensing with mercy, according to what is written, "Preserve mercy and justice, and ever draw near to God."[9] God loves mercy and justice; therefore, the one who practices mercy and justice draws near to God. It follows that every person should make a thorough self-examination. The rich should carefully consider their means, from which they intend to make offerings, in order to make certain that they have not wielded power over the poor, or used force against the weak, or committed extortion against those in a subordinate position. We are commanded to maintain justice and equity even toward slaves. Do not use force because you rule, nor commit extortion because you are able to do so, but show the qualities of justice even while the means of authority are available to you. It is no proof of reverence for God if you obey when you cannot do otherwise, but rather when you have the ability to transgress, and do not. If, after taking what belongs to the poor, you give back to the poor, you should know that it would have been better if you had neither extorted from them nor given to them.

[6]Prov 3.9 LXX.
[7]Prov 15.8 LXX.
[8]Mal 3.8, 10 LXX.
[9]Hos 12.6 LXX.

Why do you taint your wealth, contaminating it with unjust gains? Why do you make your offering an abomination, attempting to show mercy to one poor person by offering what you have taken from another through injustice? Show mercy rather to the one you have wronged. Lavish your kindness on that person; give to the one you have wronged, and you will fulfill mercy with justice. God has nothing to do with greed; neither is the Lord a companion of thieves and extortioners. It is not because God is powerless to feed the poor that he has left them for us to care for, but rather because he desires that we should be fruitful in justice and kindness through our own good works. Mercy does not come from injustice, nor blessing from a curse, nor goodness from tears. God says to those who cause the tears of the oppressed, "What I hate, you do; you cover my altar with tears, weeping and groaning."[10] Show mercy from your own earnings, and not from injustice; do not even think of bringing unjust gains to God under the pretext of showing mercy. Such displays are empty glory. They focus on the things that bring human praise, not the praise that comes from God. For this reason, the Lord well said, "Beware of practicing your piety before others in order to be seen by them."[11] If you wish to perform works of mercy in the sight of God, take care not to do so out of greedy gains, knowing that God takes no joy in beholding such things.

This is the reason we perform works of mercy: in order to receive back mercy from God. God gives back to those he approves, and he approves no greedy person. Gifts offered to God are no gifts at all if in acquiring them you have made your brother or sister sorrowful. The Lord says, "When you are offering your gift at the altar, if you remember that your brother or sister has something against you, leave your gift there before the altar and go; first be reconciled to your brother or sister, and then come and offer your gift."[12] Remember Zacchaeus the tax collector, who proposed to give back fourfold

[10]Mal 2.13 LXX.
[11]Mt 6.1.
[12]Mt 5.23–24.

if he had defrauded anyone of anything, as well as distributing half of his remaining possessions to the poor. He wished to receive Christ as a guest, and he knew that Christ would not accept his extravagance towards the poor unless he first gave back the gains taken from others through injustice. Thus, Christ also received his sincere amendment, and said, "Today, salvation has come to this house."[13] This example was given for all those who do works of mercy, but do not first seek to reestablish equity. But to those who guard against injustice while neglecting to practice mercy, it is said, "Every tree that does not bear good fruit is cut down and thrown into the fire."[14] Such a tree will never be pleasing to the heavenly gardener, who said, "I came seeking fruit and found none," and thus commanded that it should be cut down, so as not to use up the soil.[15]

It is also apparent that anyone who does not return an item taken from the poor as a pledge is condemned by God; a terrible judgment is pronounced against such a person: "The one who has not received back a pledge will cry out to me, and I will listen, for I am merciful."[16] According to the Law, it was not permitted to glean one's fields, or make a second pass through the vineyards, or thoroughly beat the fruit from the olive trees.[17] These were to be left for the poor. If such commands were given to those under the Law, what shall we say of those who are in Christ? To them the Lord says, "Unless your righteousness exceeds that of the scribes and Pharisees, you will never enter the kingdom of heaven."[18] For this reason, the Apostle exhorts us to give to those who have nothing not only out of our crops and produce, but also from the works of our hands. "Do good work with your hands, so that you may have something to give to those in need."[19]

[13] Lk 19.9.
[14] Mt 3.10.
[15] Cf. Lk 13.6–9.
[16] Ex 22.27 LXX.
[17] Cf. Deut 24.19–22.
[18] Mt 5.20.
[19] Eph 4.28.

To those who wished to follow him, the Lord introduced the practice of selling all one's property for the benefit of the poor, and so to follow him in this way. To his perfect followers, he enjoined the entire and complete fulfillment of mercy, so that, having finished their service to others by means of possessions, they might embark upon service by means of word and spirit. To the rest, he ordained allotment and sharing of what they have, so that in this way they might be seen as imitators of the kindness of God, showing mercy and giving and sharing. As the Scripture says, "Give, and it will be given to you."[20] By such acts God promised that they would become his companions. These are the ones who stand at the Lord's right hand, to whom the King says when he appears, "Come, you that are blessed by my Father, inherit the kingdom prepared for you from the foundation of the world; for I was hungry and you gave me food, I was thirsty and you gave me something to drink, I was a stranger and you welcomed me, I was naked and you gave me clothing, I was sick and in prison, and you came to me."[21] Then the righteous will be amazed and say, "When did we do this for you, Lord?" And he will say to them, "Truly I tell you, just as you did it to one of the least of these my brothers and sisters, you did it to me."[22] Eagerness to serve holy people is accounted as reverence for Christ, and the one who eagerly ministers to the poor is shown to be a companion of Christ. This is the case not only of those who divest themselves of a great amount, but also of those who bring forward some small thing, even if they give only a cup of cold water to a disciple in the name of a disciple.[23] The disciples' poverty, as the world considers it, is an opportunity for you to acquire true wealth, you rich people. Through such actions you will become co-workers of Christ. You feed soldiers of Christ, and do so freely, not under any compulsion. The Heavenly King does not use compulsion, nor does he demand payment, but

[20]Lk 6.38.
[21]Mt 25.34–36.
[22]Mt 25.40.
[23]Cf. Mt 10.42.

accepts those who serve eagerly, so that in giving they may receive, and in showing honor they may be honored, and in sharing what is temporal they may be invited to share in what is eternal.

These things should be a constant reminder to us; we should place them before the very eyes of our soul, so that we may not neglect the opportune moment, nor pass over the present time, waiting for some other chance, lest we should be lost in the end on account of our hesitation and delaying. May the Lord grant that we may be found fruitful and vigilant, mindful of his commands, ready and unimpeded at his glorious appearing; in Christ himself our God, to whom be glory, might, and honor, together with the Father and the Holy Spirit, now and always, and forever and ever. Amen.

Bibliography

Texts

Courtonne, Yves, ed. and trans. *Saint Basile: Homélies sur la richesse: edition critique et exégétique.* Paris: Firmin-Didot, 1935.

Migne, J.P. et al, ed. *Patrologia Graeca* 31. Paris: Migne, 1857 (cited as PG).

Translations

Butterworth, G.W., trans. "The Rich Man's Salvation." In *Clement of Alexandria*, G. W. Butterworth, trans. Loeb Classical Library 92. Cambridge, MS: Harvard University Press, 1919.

Browne, Charles Gordon, and James Edward Swallow. *Select Orations of St Gregory Nazianzen.* Nicene and Post-Nicene Fathers ser. 2 vol. 7. Oxford: Parker, 1894 (series cited as NPNF).

Chrestou, Panagiotis K., trans. (modern Greek). *M. Basileiou Erga.* Hellenes Pateres tes Ekklesias 7. Thessalonike: Paterikai Ekdoseis "Gregorios ho Palamas," 1973.

Corrigan, Kevin, trans. *The Life of St Macrina.* Saskatoon, Saskatchewan: Perigrina Publishing Co., 1987.

Harrison, Nonna Verna, trans. *St Basil the Great: On the Human Condition.* Crestwood, NY: St Vladimir's Seminary Press, 2005.

Holman, Susan R., trans. "In Time of Famine and Drought [Tempore famis et siccitatis]." *The Hungry Are Dying: Beggars and Bishops in Roman Cappadocia.* By Susan R. Holman. New York: Oxford University Press, 2001.

Jackson, Blomfield, trans. *St Basil: Letters and Select Works.* NPNF ser. 2 vol. 8. Oxford: Parker, 1895.

Moore, William, and Henry Austin Wilson, trans. *Select Writings and Letters of Gregory, Bishop of Nyssa.* NPNF ser. 2 vol. 5. Oxford: Parker, 1893.

Robertson, Archibald, trans. *Select Writings and Letters of Athanasius, Bishop of Alexandria.* NPNF ser. 2 vol. 4. Oxford: Parker, 1892.

Roth, Catharine P. trans. *St John Chrysostom: On Wealth and Poverty.* Crestwood, NY: St Vladimir's Seminary Press, 1984.

Toal, M.F., trans. *The Sunday Sermons of the Great Fathers.* Vol. 3. Chicago: Regnery, 1959.

Wagner, Sr M. Monica, trans. *St Basil: Ascetical Works.* Fathers of the Church 9. Washington, DC: Catholic University Press, 1962.

Way, Sr Agnes Clare, trans. *Saint Basil: Exegetic Homilies.* Fathers of the Church 46. Washington, DC: Catholic University Press, 1963.

Studies

Chrestou, Panagiotis K. *Ho Megas Vasileios: Vios kai Politeia, Syngrammata, Theologike Skepsis.* Thessalonike: Patriarchikon Hidryma Paterikon Meleton, 1978.

Constantelos, Demetrios J. "St Basil the Great's Social Thought and Involvement." *Greek Orthodox Theological Review* 26 (1981): 81–86.

Ibid. *Byzantine Philanthropy and Social Welfare.* New Brunswick, NJ: Rutgers University Press, 1968.

Finley, Moses I. *Ancient Slavery and Modern Ideology.* New York: Viking Press, 1980.

Gould, Graham. "Basil of Caesarea and the Problem of the Wealth of Monasteries." In *The Church and Wealth: Papers Read at the 1986 Summer Meeting and the 1987 Winter Meeting of the Ecclesiastical History Society.* W. J. Sheils and Diana Wood, ed. New York: B. Blackwell, 1987.

Gribomont, Jean. "Monasticism and Asceticism." In *Christian Spirituality: Origins to the Twelfth Century.* Bernard McGinn, John Meyendorff, and Jean Leclercq, eds. New York: Crossroad, 1985.

Hanrahan, James. *St Basil the Great (329–379): A Life with Excerpts from His Works.* Toronto: Basilian Press, 1979. ‹http://www.basilian.org/ basil_complete_en.php› March 23, 2007.

van den Hoek, Annewies. "Widening the Eye of the Needle: Wealth and Poverty in the Works of Clement of Alexandria." In *Wealth and Poverty in Early Church and Society.* Susan R. Holman, ed. Grand Rapids, MI: Baker Academic and Brookline, MA: Holy Cross Orthodox Press, 2008.

Holman, Susan R. *The Hungry Are Dying: Beggars and Bishops in Roman Cappadocia*. New York: Oxford University Press, 2001.

Jones, A.H.M. *The Later Roman Empire 284–602: A Social Economic and Administrative Survey,* Vol. II. Norman, OK: University of Oklahoma Press, 1964.

Karayannopoulos, Ioannes. "St Basil's Social Activity: Principles and Praxis." In *Basil of Caesarea: Christian, Humanist, Ascetic: A Sixteen-Hundredth Anniversary Symposium*. Paul Jonathan Fedwick, ed. Toronto: Pontifical Institute of Mediaeval Studies, 1981.

Kopecek, Thomas A. "The Social Class of the Cappadocian Fathers." *Church History* 42 (1973): 453–66.

Rousseau, Philip. *Basil of Caesarea*. Berkeley: University of California Press, 1998.

Salzman, Michele Renee. *The Making of a Christian Aristocracy: Social and Religious Change in the Western Roman Empire*. Cambridge, MA: Harvard University Press, 2002.

Siepierski, Paolo. "Poverty and Spirituality: St Basil and Liberation Theology." *Greek Orthodox Theological Review* 33 (1998): 313–26.

POPULAR PATRISTICS SERIES

ST VLADIMIR'S SEMINARY PRESS
1-800-204-2665 • www.svspress.com